T0168041

It Won't Be Long Now

It Won't Be Long Now

The Diary of a Hong Kong Prisoner of War

Graham Heywood

Edited by G.C. Emerson

BLACKSMITH BOOKS

Dedicated to all the POWs of Sham Shui Po Camp

It Won't Be Long Now
ISBN 978-988-13765-1-0

Published by Blacksmith Books
Unit 26, 19/F, Block B, Wah Lok Industrial Centre,
37-41 Shan Mei Street, Fo Tan, Hong Kong
Tel: (+852) 2877 7899
www.blacksmithbooks.com

Copyright © 2015 The estate of Graham Heywood

All rights reserved. No part of this publication may be
reproduced, stored or transmitted in any form or by any means,
electronic, mechanical, photocopying, recording or otherwise,
without the prior written permission of the publisher.

Also by Graham Heywood:
Rambles in Hong Kong
Hongkong Typhoons

Contents

CAMPS IN THE FAR EAST.

P W   PRISONER OF WAR CAMP
C I   CIVILIAN INTERNMENT CAMP
C A   CIVILIAN ASSEMBLY CENTRE

U.S.S.R.

MANCHURIA
[MANCHUKUO]

MUKDEN [HOTEN] P W

Peking

Vladivostok

KEIJO P W
JINSEN DIV.
P W

KOREA
[CHOSEN]

JAPAN

Tokyo

Osaka KOBE [1 & 2]
ZENTSUJI   P W

HAKODATE GROUP
P W CAMPS

TOKYO GROUP
C I CAMPS

URAWA
SUMIRE GAUKIN

TOKYO GROUP
P W CAMPS

KAWASAKI
SHINAGANA
KANAGAWA
CENTRAL PARK
   YOKOHAMA
HIRAOKA
OMORI

OSAKA GROUP
P W CAMPS

AMAGASAKI
HARIMA
KAWASAKI
KOBE
SAKURAJIMA
OSAKA DOCKS

FUKUOKA GROUP
P W CAMPS
UBE
MOTOYAMA
MUKOJIMA
HIGASHIMISOME
INNOSHIMA
OHAMA
OMINE

CHINA

CHEFOO SHANTUNG   C A
WEIHSIEN SHANTUNG   C A
TSINGTAO SHANTUNG   C A
YANGCHOW KIANGSU   C A

SHANGHAI GROUP
C A CENTRES
Shanghai

HAIPHONG RD.,
SHANGHAI   C I

P.O. BOX 106,
SHANGHAI   P W

CHAPEI
COLUMBIA CLUB
GT. WESTERN RD.
LUNGHWA
YU-YUEN RD.
POOTUNG

AMOY, C I
Amoy

CANTON C I
Canton

Hong Kong

FORMOSA
[TAIWAN]

TAIWAN GROUP P W CAMPS
TAIHOKU
KARENKO
TAMAZO

Tropic of Cancer

BURMA

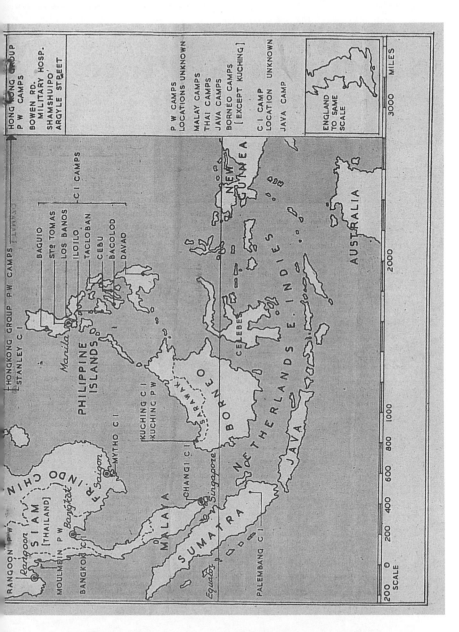

From the April 1944 issue of the Far East Special Monthly Edition of *The Prisoner of War*, published by the Prisoner of War Department of the Red Cross and St. John War Organisation *[1] (see page 186 for image credits)*

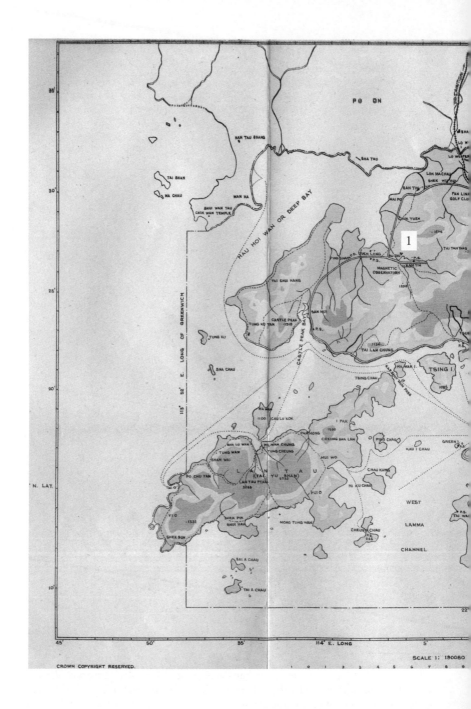

CROWN COPYRIGHT RESERVED.

SCALE 1: 190080

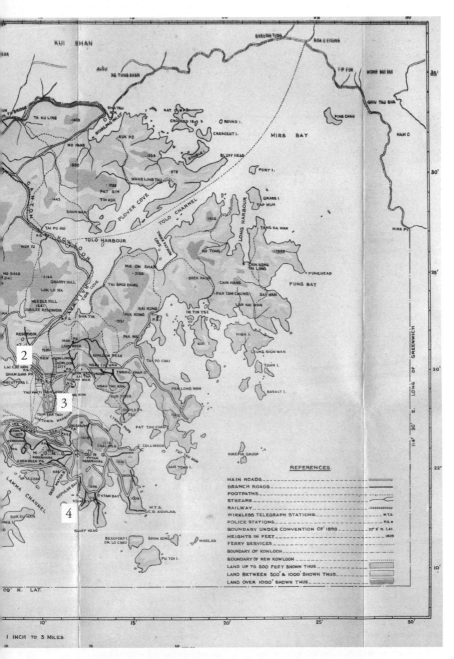

Map of Hong Kong from the *Hong Kong Yearbook* 1947
1. Au Tau; 2. Sham Shui Po; 3. Observatory; 4. Stanley

BASIC SYMBOLS:

Battalion	II	Airborne		
Regiment	III	Air Force unit		
Brigade	x	Armor		
Division, air division	xx	Artillery		
Corps	xxx	Cavalry		
Army, air force	xxxx	Infantry		
Army group	xxxxx			

Examples of Combinations of Basic Symbols:

Small British infantry detachment   Br. ⊠

34th Regimental Combat Team   34 RCT

Combat Command C of 1st Armored Division   C ⊡ 1

82d Airborne Division   82

1st Motorized Division   ⊠ 1 Mtz.

2d Marine Division   2 Mar.

French Second Corps less detachments   FR ⊡ (−)

Third Army   THIRD

First Air Force   FIRST

12th Army Group, commanded by Bradley    12 BRADLEY

OTHER SYMBOLS:

	Actual location	Prior location		
Troops on the march			Troops displacing and direction	
Troops in position			Troops in position under attack	
Troops in bivouac or reserve			Route of march or flight	
	Occupied	Unoccupied	Boundary between units	——— xxx ——— (Appropriate basic symbol)
Field works			Fort	
Strong prepared positions			Fortified area	

Hong Kong—consisting of the island of that name, Kowloon Peninsula, and leased territory on the Chinese mainland—was acquired by Great Britain in 1841. It gradually became an international shipping center and a symbol of British influence in the Far East. In 1941, Hong Kong was not so important militarily to Japan as it was politically: should the British be forcibly ejected from the colony, it would mean a serious loss of face for them in the Orient. This was well understood by the British who, though regarding the colony as an untenable outpost, recognized that the harbor should be denied to the Japanese as long as possible. Two Canadian infantry battalions were sent to the colony in November, 1941, as a calculated show of force, making a total of six battalions available for defense.

The British plan of defense envisioned occupation of the Gin Drinker's Line (center) by three battalions, while the other three occupied beach defense positions on Hong Kong Island. It was recognized that the mainland line was too long to be manned in sufficient strength to repel a strong attack; but the three battalions were expected to hold for about a week before withdrawing to the island, where the main battle would be fought. The island had twenty-nine coastal guns, some of which could fire on mainland targets, but only token naval forces (one destroyer, eight torpedo boats, and four gunboats) remained in Hong Kong waters after war broke out. The army troops, only partially trained, were short of transport and lacked adequate mortar ammunition. But the greatest armament weakness was in aircraft—the garrison had only six obsolete planes. The Japanese were undoubtedly familiar with British military defense measures, for in the prewar months the members of the Japanese Consulate moved about freely, and unhindered traffic to and from the mainland facilitated the activities of Japanese agents.

In November, 1941, the British commander moved the three mainland defense battalions from training camps into the Gin Drinker's Line, where they set to work improving the defenses. By this time, a false sense of confidence existed among the troops and many of the civilians. The island was impregnable, it was said, and the Japanese equipment, troops, and tactics were decidedly inferior; they were inept at night operations, and their aircraft were obsolete. Nor was British intelligence on 7 December very reliable: reports of 20,000 Japanese concentrating near Sham Chun Hu (top center) were discounted. Actually, this was the Japanese 38th Division, preparing to attack across the border. Fortunately, the British commander, Maj. Gen. C. M. Maltby, took no risks and manned all his defenses.

About 0800, 8 December, the Japanese struck without warning. Air raids destroyed the British aircraft, and concurrently the Japanese 38th Division moved across the border toward the Gin Drinker's Line. By dusk, 9 December, they were probing the British position. That night, their strength massed in the west, they ripped a hole in the defenses by seizing and holding the key strong point, Shing Mun Redoubt. The British failed to make any counterattack to recapture the redoubt, and, on the 10th, the Japanese exploited their success by widening the gap and forcing a British withdrawal. On 11 December, with his troops being driven southward, Maltby ordered a withdrawal to the island. By the 13th, it had been successfully executed. That day, and again on the 15th, the Japanese summoned Maltby to surrender and, upon being refused, unleashed intensive artillery and aerial bombardments. On the night of 18 December, the 38th Division crossed to the island as shown. By nightfall of the 19th, they had split the defenders in two groups—Maltby had erred in failing to hold the key Wong Nai Chong Gap (lower right) in strength, and his belated counterattacks were unavailing. By the 24th, their water supply almost exhausted, the disorganized British were beaten. On Christmas Day, Maltby surrendered.

In just eighteen days, an efficient, well-trained, and adequately led Japanese division, supported by an equally effective air force and navy, had overrun the stately British crown colony. Its total casualties were 2,754; the British lost 11,848.

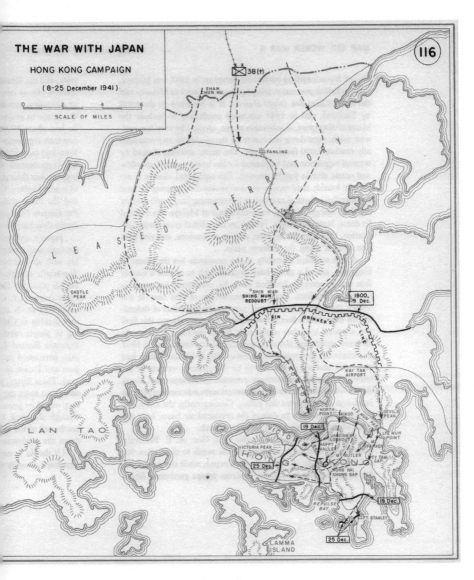

THE WAR WITH JAPAN

HONG KONG CAMPAIGN

(8-25 December 1941)

SCALE OF MILES

Above: Map printed in 1959 and originally bound into a book for use by West
Point cadets in the late 1950s
Facing page: Key and map description

FOREWORD

By Shun Chi Ming, Director of the Hong Kong Observatory

The idea of publishing this manuscript stemmed from my first visit back in November 2012 to Mr John Peacock, the last Director of the Hong Kong Observatory (1981-84) from England. During the visit, John told me many things about the good old days of the Observatory since he first joined as Scientific Officer in 1950. These of course included his memories of Mr Graham Heywood who was the first Director after the Second World War and led the re-building of the Observatory. The first thing I learnt was that Mr Heywood came from a very eminent family. John also showed me his photo albums with many pictures of the Observatory, and one of them caught my attention – a staff photo taken outside the Director's quarters in 1955 on the retirement of Mr Heywood – and John told me who was who in the picture: Frank Apps, Colin Ramage, Northan Lawrence, Pat Goodfellow. Most of these names I had never heard before. This was really great!

When I visited Mr Peacock again in January 2013, he gave me a photocopy of a manuscript authored by Mr Heywood entitled *It Won't Be Long Now*. It was a typescript of Heywood's diary about his internment at the Sham Shui Po Prisoner-of-War (POW) camp during the Second World War. John told me that the main body of this manuscript had never been released by the Heywood family, considering the hardship and even humiliation of the POWs described in the diary. John offered to write to Mr Michael Knight, son-in-law of Mr Heywood and widower of Susan, the elder daughter of Mr Heywood, and Ms Veronica Heywood, the younger sister of Susan, to secure the family's consent for the release of the diary.

On the flight from London back to Hong Kong, I read from beginning to end the whole manuscript. Thanks to the excellent writing of Mr Heywood, it was really a treat to read it. Apart from telling many stories about the prolonged hardships, adversities, survival from malnutrition and diseases, and the repeated hopes of liberation that failed to materialize (thus the title of the diary *It Won't Be Long Now*), that he experienced as a POW in the camp, the diary also reflects Heywood's highly positive attitudes to life and his strong sense of humour overcoming the hardships, and perhaps also his enlightenment learnt from the internment. For example:

> *"Len and I had hopes of being sent to the civilian internment camp at Stanley, on the south side of Hong Kong Island, where all the British non-combatants were confined. In spite of our protests, however, the Japs throughout treated us as prisoners of war, and on arrival at Sham Shui Po we were dumped in the middle of the road with the other prisoners. The officers were detailed off to their quarters, the Royal Scots to their lines, the Canadian to his; the Indians were conducted to the far corner of the camp, and we two were left standing in the road with 'no home, no momma, no poppa, no chow', as the little Chinese beggar-boys say."*

> *"During the war a party of R.A.M.C. men were rounded up by the Japanese, who, to save the trouble of taking them into captivity, beheaded them all save one. The latter, a Corporal Leath, was left for dead on the ground, with a severe wound on the back of his neck. He*

was subsequently taken to hospital, where he made a complete recovery, and served as an orderly during the latter part of his imprisonment. The following verse, which he wrote in somebody's autograph book, shows the light-hearted way in which people put up with things ...

> *'I nearly lost my head by Gad;*
> *I sometimes wish I really had;*
> *But luckily I lost no teeth.*
> *Yours sincerely,*
> *N.J. Leath.'"*

"*Then again, we were not going to ask too much of life. When the war was over, we told ourselves, we would never again sigh for the moon. We had discovered that we could do perfectly well without luxuries, and we could be content with the simple things of life ... good food, decent living conditions, and the companionship of our families. We began to realize that happiness depended very little on material possessions; the loss of all our worldly goods counted for nothing compared with the loss of freedom, home life and useful employment. Life had been getting too complicated; we would surely be more grateful for the simple things.*"

"*It did not do to take too much thought for the morrow; better to try to live a good life each day for its own sake, and not for any vague rewards in some future existence ... anyway rather an unworthy motive, I had always thought. There was a meaning to life, here and now, ... 'love thy neighbor as thyself' ... and there was one stronghold sure which would not fail me, the love of dear ones waiting for me at home. Perhaps we were unlucky to be born into this era of upheaval; perhaps though, our generation would have outstanding opportunities of shaping a better world.*"

"Accounts of life in the internment camp differed widely. One friend, an enthusiastic biologist, was full of his doings; he had grown champion vegetables, had seen all sort of rare birds (including vultures, after the corpses) and had run a successful yeast brewery. Altogether, he said, it had been a great experience ... a bit too long, perhaps, but not bad fun at all. Another ended up her account by saying 'Oh, Mr. Heywood, it was hell on earth'. It all depended on their point of view."

These are indeed words of wisdom. Here in Hong Kong, we have continued to enjoy freedom, peaceful times and abundance in material wealth since the War, but perhaps we may not have recognized the fortunate environment we are in, and could choose to be content with the simple things of life. Heywood's words are truly food for thought for all of us today – in the midst of political unrest, global warming and increasing consumerism, but decreasing spiritual satisfaction and happiness.

Very soon, Michael and Veronica were contacted and had agreed to the release of the manuscript. We also started to discuss the possibility of publishing the diary. Meanwhile, they were very kind to donate an original typescript of the diary to the Observatory – it was on display at the 130th anniversary exhibition for the Observatory at the Hong Kong Museum of History in the summer of 2013, and is now on permanent display at the Observatory's History Room. Veronica even flew all the way from Dublin, Ireland to join a reunion dinner in November 2013 with present and retired colleagues. During that occasion, she also caught up with her childhood friend Mr LAU Tin-chi who is now a celebrity – an experienced TV producer and still an active radio broadcaster. Tin-chi is the son of Mr LAU Pak-wa, Special Clerk of the Observatory who worked with Mr Heywood for many years before and after the War. Veronica and Tin-chi were childhood friends in the 1950s due to the Observatory connection and today, more than 60 years afterwards, Tin-chi still has many fond memories and photos of the Heywood family to share with us.

At this juncture I must mention Geoffrey Emerson, who was Vice Principal of St Paul's College on Bonham Road, Hong Kong, where I was a schoolboy. He is also the author of the book *Hong Kong Internment, 1942-1945: Life in the Japanese Civilian Camp at Stanley*. Frankly speaking I knew little about Geoff before and even did not know about his book. At St Paul's College I did not have the chance to be taught by him, and the interactions with him that I could remember were discussions on student disciplinary matters when I was the College's Head Prefect before graduation. When I really got to know him was, interestingly, almost 30 years later, after I learnt that he wrote the book on the Stanley internment camp. I approached him with the hope that I could learn something more about another ex-Director, Mr Benjamin Evans, who was interned at Stanley during the War. Indeed, through Geoff I was connected with a lady in her 90s in England. She had been interned in Stanley Camp and had known Mr Evans. Barbara Redwood Anslow remembered him well, and when I visited her in November 2012, she showed me her diary record about their encounter at a hotel (actually a brothel with very poor conditions for temporary internment of the civilians before moving to Stanley) in January 1942: "One evening a Mr Evans from the Royal Observatory gave us a lecture on the stars, on the roof". What an amazing story this was!

But the adventure did not stop there – considering Geoff's expertise and wealth of knowledge on internment camps during the War and his long association with the Hong Kong Branch of the Royal Asiatic Society (RAS), I consulted him for his advice on the possibility of publishing Mr Heywood's diary. Geoff was very forthcoming and initiated dialogues with key members of the RAS on the publication. It turned out that while the diary would fit rather nicely into the subjects of interest to the RAS, the size of the diary did not fall into the category supported for publication. It was a bit disappointing to me but we had never assumed that it would be easy to get the war diary published.

But we persevered... and Geoff made many good suggestions to add value to the book which could attract a readership. He found a capable friend, Yvonne LAI Siu Mei, who very kindly typed up the whole manuscript in electronic format to facilitate subsequent editing. Enhancing the visual content would be very important, Geoff told me. Fortunately, again thanks to the 130th anniversary exhibition for the Observatory, I had been seeking the help of collectors in Hong Kong to provide historical photos of typhoons, heavy rains and of course the Observatory itself for the exhibition. One by one I managed to gather interesting photos that were related in some way to the diary: photos of the Sham Shui Po military camp itself, photos of the Japanese invasion of Hong Kong, journals on the internment camps published during the War, photos of the old Sacred Hill which was levelled by the Japanese deploying internees from Sham Shui Po, including Mr Heywood himself, a photo of the Peninsula Hotel still painted in camouflage colours, where Mr Heywood had stayed for a couple of weeks after his liberation before heading back to England, and even an aerial photo of an air-raid by US B-24 bombers on 16 October 1944 which was actually described in the diary, and so on... My special thanks go to Mr Tim KO Tim Keung, who is a very good friend of Geoff and a local historian passionate about the history of Hong Kong, for contributing the largest number of photos, including some very rare photos of the Japanese invasion; Messrs William TONG, Ricky YAM, James NG and SIU Him Fung who are all active members of the Hong Kong Collectors Society; and to the members of the Gwulo historical Hong Kong website. Meanwhile, I have picked up the hobby of historical photo collection in the process and so have managed to contribute a few to this book myself.

Finally, but certainly not the least, and again thanks to Geoff's introduction, we met with Pete Spurrier of Blacksmith Books in early

February 2015, in a coffee house down the hill of the Observatory, to see if he would be interested in publishing the book. This took place just before my trip to England to visit the Heywood family in Hampshire to learn more about Mr Heywood and to examine his photo albums and archives more closely. Unexpectedly, Pete agreed to publish the book on the spot – a very welcome surprise. Pete also reminded us that 2015 was the 70th anniversary of the end of the Second World War and so it would be perfect timing for publishing the war diary. Indeed it was also perfect timing for me to "seal the deal" by bringing a copy of the publication agreement to Hampshire for signature by the Heywood family.

Once again, I wish to express my deepest appreciation to all those mentioned above who have helped in making this publication a reality! My biggest thanks of course go to Geoff who not only guided me through the whole process and connected me with all the key people supporting the publication, but also kindly agreed to serve as editor for the book. I would also like to thank the Heywood family, in particular Veronica and Michael, for agreeing to release the diary in the first place, and for their trust in me to take forward the publication, and also Ms Bridget West, daughter of Susan and Michael, who helped a great deal in managing the photos and archives of Mr Heywood and scanning them for the book.

I hope you as the reader will enjoy reading Mr Heywood's diary, and in the process learn a bit more about Hong Kong during wartime.

SHUN Chi Ming
Hong Kong
April 2015

Biography of Graham Heywood

By Veronica Heywood[1], SHUN Chi Ming[2] and Geoffrey Charles Emerson[3]

Graham Scudamore Percival Heywood, MA, FRMetS, was born on 5 July 1903. He was the son of Lt-Col Gerald Graham Percival Heywood and Mary nee Stanhope. He married Valerie Rose Isabel Wyatt, daughter of Lt-Col John Railton Wyatt, on 4 June 1937. They had two daughters: Susan Mary born in Kowloon Hospital, Hong Kong, in July 1938 and Veronica Anne born in Melbourne, Australia, in February 1942. He died on 23 January 1985 peacefully at home, at Critchells, Lockerley, Hampshire, UK.

Mr Heywood was educated at Winchester College, Winchester, Hampshire. His house-master inspired his lifelong love of mountain climbing. He graduated from New College, Oxford University in 1925 with a Bachelor of Arts (BA). He sculled and coxed New College Eight in rowing and represented his college at Henley Regatta. He was also an excellent marksman and competed at the National Shooting Centre in Bisley, Surrey, but disagreed with any form of game shooting. He had a

---

1 Ms Veronica Heywood is daughter of Graham Heywood

2 Mr Chi Ming Shun is the current Director of the Hong Kong Observatory (2011-)

3 Mr Geoffrey Charles Emerson is author of the book *Hong Kong Internment, 1942-1945: Life in the Japanese Civilian Camp at Stanley* and also was a teacher at St Paul's College, Hong Kong

fine tenor voice. He graduated from New College, Oxford University in 1926 with a Bachelor of Science (BSc). He graduated from New College, Oxford University in 1934 with a Master of Arts (MA). His BSc paper on motions of electrons in air was subsequently published in the Royal Society Journal.

Mr Heywood taught Science at Radley College briefly after graduating from university in the autumn of 1925. He joined the Territorial Army's Officers Training Corps on 23 December 1926. He was signed on as meteorologist to an expedition to the Antarctic that never got off the ground due to lack of sponsorship during the recession. He studied the movement of air in hilly country at a research station in the Cotswolds commissioned by the 'War Office', as it was then called, to find out what would happen should poison gas be used in similar circumstances in future battles. His findings about the inversion of temperature and risks of frost damage proved to be of great use to fruit growers. He was a lifelong supporter of the Boy Scouts and was presented with the Silver Acorn by Queen Elizabeth II for his commitment on Saint George's Day at Windsor Castle in 1969.

Mr Heywood joined the Royal Observatory Hong Kong as Professional Assistant on 10 August 1932. The job appealed to his sense of adventure. He was married to Valerie in 1937 in St Andrew's Church, Kowloon, where their first child Susan Mary was christened.

In 1940 the family followed government advice and evacuated to Australia. Mr Heywood settled his daughter and wife, who was expecting her second child, in Melbourne and returned to his work in Hong Kong. In December 1941 when the Japanese attacked Hong Kong, Mr Heywood and a colleague, Leonard Starbuck, went at 11 a.m. on 8 December to Au Tau in the New Territories, near the border, to dismantle the magnetic station and collect the instruments and equipment there. At about 3 p.m. they were ready to return to Kowloon when they were captured by Japanese soldiers. They were not to return to the Observatory until the

The Heywood family in the early 1950s (with Veronica sitting on the ground and Susan sitting on the step) *[2]*

war ended. After being held in various places in the New Territories, on 8 January 1942 they were taken by lorry to Sham Shui Po, where they were to spend the next three-and-a-half years in the military Prisoner-of-War camp. The Director of the Royal Observatory, Benjamin D. Evans, was incarcerated in Stanley Internment Camp for civilians on Hong Kong Island, but the Japanese refused to allow Heywood and Starbuck to join the civilians there. They were not to meet Mr Evans again until 29 August 1945, at Stanley. On 18 September 1945, Mr Heywood sailed from Hong Kong on the HMS *Glengyle* and transferred to the P&O ship *Maloja* at Colombo, Ceylon, arriving in October at Southampton.

His wife Valerie, who had been evacuated from Hong Kong to Australia and had gone to England during the war, was waiting for him on the dock. His two daughters, Susan and Veronica (who had yet to meet her father as she was born in Australia shortly after he was captured) watched the ship as it sailed slowly up the Solent from their grandparents' attic window.

Heywood took up the post of Director of the Royal Observatory on 18 May 1946 after returning to Hong Kong, having recovered after six months' leave. His wife and two daughters followed him shortly afterwards. A couple of days after his return, his former cook from before the war, Ah Bing, arrived to offer his services again. Heywood was Director until 1955. During this time he volunteered to form and lead several scout groups, while his wife volunteered in the Kowloon Welfare Centre of the Hong Kong Society for the Protection of Children.

The Heywood family on vacation at a bungalow on Sunset Peak, Lantau Island. Veronica (left) and Susan (right) with Heather and Chris Goodfellow (centre, front row), children of Heywood's colleague Pat Goodfellow

The family spent holidays in the heat of the summer at cooler altitudes underneath Sunset Peak on Lantau Island. Heywood's holiday was on several occasions interrupted when he was called back with great urgency to the Observatory to attend to his duties before the approach of typhoons. He and his friend, the botanist Dr Geoffrey Herklots[4], would lead plant-hunting and bird-watching expeditions into the hills. Heywood was author of the books *Rambles in Hong Kong* published by the South China Morning Post in 1938 and *Hongkong Typhoons* published by the Royal Observatory in 1950. The 1992 version of *Rambles in Hong Kong* with a new introduction and commentary by Richard Gee provides more reminiscences of Mr Heywood during his Hong Kong days.

Rough cover design by Veronica Heywood for the 1992 edition of *Rambles in Hong Kong*

On his retirement in 1955 (see newspaper cuttings and staff photo on following pages), Mr Heywood returned to England, moving from his family home near Much Wenlock in Shropshire to be near his daughters who were at boarding school in the south of England. He and his wife set about preparing a beautiful garden with shrubbery, herbaceous borders, a rose garden, croquet and tennis courts, a goldfish pond, a rockery, a paved terrace, an orchard and a vegetable patch. Always a scientist, he planted a rain gauge in the middle of the lawn, thermometers in the porch and a barometer in the hall. Readings were taken daily and if Mr Heywood had to go away for any length of time, he left his daughters with strict instructions to take the readings for him.

It took him no time before he had started up a scout group in Lockerley village, organising adventure camps for the group in the New Forest and

---

4 Dr Herklots was also Secretary for Development, head of the predecessor of the Department of Agriculture, Fisheries and Forestry, during 1946-1950.

progressed to running Jamborees for thousands of Boy Scouts. He served as warden in the village church and took up bell ringing (campanology). As a result of suffering from malaria during his internment, Mr Heywood always became feverish whenever he caught a common cold and he never regained his former physique.

Family holidays would be spent anywhere where there were mountains: Switzerland, Scotland, Wales and the western mountains of Ireland. He always loved to plan expeditions up Ireland's highest peaks, Carrantuohill and Brandon Mountain in Kerry, and travels to Nyasaland as it was then called, now Malawi, where his eldest daughter Susan had joined her husband Michael Knight. When Susan's husband took up a post in Washington DC, Mr and Mrs Heywood travelled to see them. They also frequently visited Ireland where their younger daughter Veronica was living.

The great joy of Mr Heywood's retirement was when he and his wife spent time with his grandchildren Nicola, Tim, Deborah and Bridget. They would recruit them into harvesting fruit, cutting down storm damaged branches and other country tasks, instilling in them all a great love of nature.

The low-cost in-house developed satellite reception system which delivered world-class satellite images as early as 1966

He always thoroughly enjoyed visits from his old Observatory colleagues. His face would light up when, on a visit, Mr Gordon Bell, whom Heywood had preceded as Director, told him of the satellite tracking equipment Bell had invented for the use of the Observatory.

Mr Heywood all his life never lost his scientific curiosity and when everyone else was complaining about freezing taps and burst pipes, he was excited at the recording of all-time lows, or the phenomena of recording identical air temperatures for both midsummer and midwinter. Mr Heywood was also talented in other subjects: he drew all the illustrations in his book *Rambles in Hong Kong* and took up landscape painting after his retirement. He was also quite fluent in Cantonese, having been to language classes when he first arrived in Hong Kong in 1932.

Tributes sent at Mr Heywood's funeral from fellow Sham Shui Po detainees told of how he had kept everyone's spirits up with his kindnesses and encouragement. His grave is in Lockerley Churchyard with a simple headstone inscribed with his family motto 'Alte Volo' – the translation from the Latin is 'Fly High'.

Lockerley Churchyard. Inscription reads: "A full life and one of service together with his beloved wife, Valerie Rose Isabel Heywood, 2nd May 1904 - 17th August 1992"

References

1. *Burke's Peerage*
2. Archives of Winchester College and New College Oxford
3. *Rambles in Hong Kong* by GSP Heywood with a new introduction and commentary by Richard Gee, 1992

Staff photo taken outside the Director's quarters on 28 January 1955 upon Heywood's retirement (front row from left to right: Royal Navy Commander Dennis Rowe, Mr and Mrs Frank Apps, Mr and Mrs Colin Ramage, Mr

活先生退休回國紀念 一九五五年十月廿八日新時代

and Mrs Heywood, Mr and Mrs Northan Lawrence, Mr and Mrs Pattison Goodfellow and an attached military person; second row, fifth from left: Mr LAU Pak Wa, Mr John Peacock and Mr CHIN Bing Chuen)

Retirement of Mr Heywood

SOUTH CHINA MORNING POST, HONGKONG.

SOCIAL THE ROUND

COMING EVENTS

H.K. Rotary Club
Meeting

TODAY'S REMINDERS

Anniversaries and Holidays.—St. Peter's Chair at Rome.
Exhibitions.—Ganymed Facsimiles, British Council Library, Gloucester Bldg., 9 a.m.
Lectures.—"A Holiday in Holland," by Mrs P. Van Vliet, Y.W.C.A., 1, Macdonnell Road, 5 p.m.
Meetings.—Hongkong Rotary Club, The Paramount, Windsor House, 12.20 p.m.; Hongkong Reel Club, Helena May Institute, 5.30 p.m.
Miscellaneous.—China Red Cross Working Party, Sandilands Hut, 9.30 a.m.; European Y.M.C.A., 10 a.m.; Garrison Players, Reading of the Play "Relative Values," Seamen's Mission, Gloucester Road.
Moon.—Twenty-fifth Day of the Twelfth Moon.
Religious.—Bible Discussion in Dean's House, 5.45 p.m.
Socials.—Cherro Club and Nine Dragons' Whist Drives, 8 p.m.; St.

POPULAR H.K. COUPLE

Mr And Mrs G. S. P. Heywood To Leave Colony Next Month

RETURNING TO ENGLAND

Mr G. S. P. Heywood, Director of the Royal Observatory, and Mrs Heywood, are leaving Hongkong for the United Kingdom on February 11. Mr Heywood is going on long leave prior to retirement in September this year.

This popular pair will be missed by many in the Colony, especially by the Observatory staff, church workers, youth associations, social welfare workers and their many friends.

Mr Heywood was educated at Winchester College, and after taking a Physics degree at Oxford, he spent some time teaching. Deciding that he preferred a job which included some scientific research, Mr Heywood spent four years in charge of a

He is still on the Scout Council and was once Chairman of the Executive Committee of the Boy Scouts Association.

Mrs Heywood has run the Women's Guild and is a leading member of the Mothers' Union. She is also an unofficial J.P., being one of the original group of women to sit on the Bench since the inception of lay women magistrates.

Until recently, Mrs Heywood was a member of the Girl Guides' Council; the International Council of Women; the Diocesan Girls' School Council, and an executive officer of the Family Planning Association. Her greatest interest is social welfare was centred on the Society for the Protection of Children, and as branch Secretary of the Kowloon centre for the past eight years she is known to have given devoted service.

Mr Heywood said that he and his wife were very fond of Hongkong. They had found many opportunities for useful activities and had won many friends.

FAREWELL DINNER

Staff Of Observatory Fete The Heywoods

The staff of the Royal Observatory fated Mr G.S.P. Heywood, the retiring Director, and Mrs Heywood at a farewell Chinese dinner at the Chinese Civil Service Association, King's Park, last night.

Left: *South China Morning Post*, 18 January 1955; below: 21 January 1955

Mr G. S. P. Heywood the retiring Director of the Royal Observatory, and Mrs Heywood were last night feted at a Chinese dinner by the staff of the Observatory. Photograph shows Mr Heywood (left) receiving from Mr C. S. Ramage a silver cigarette case, presented by the European staff of the Observatory.—(Staff Photographer).

Farewell Party At St Andrew's

Gifts Presented To The Heywoods

Members of the congregation of St Andrew's Church bade farewell to Mr G. S. P. Heywood, the retiring Director of the Royal Observatory, and Mrs Heywood at a function in the Hall of the Church last night.

The Vicar, the Rev. J. H. Ogilvie, presented Mr Heywood with a Bible and a pipe. Mrs Heywood received a brooch.

Mrs Olive Perkins, on behalf of the Women's Guild and Mothers' Union, presented the couple with three saucepans.

Addressing the gathering, Rev. Ogilvie said that the function was being held so that members of the congregation could say farewell to "two very loyal and faithful servants of St Andrew's Church."

He added that Mr Heywood took a very great interest in the Church and also in the St Andrew's Boy Scout movement for a great number of years. Mr and Mrs Heywood would be missed very much when they left Hongkong on February 11.

Rev Ogilvie thanked Mrs Heywood for her work among the women in the congregation.

Replying, Mr Heywood said, "My wife and I are moved by the honour accorded us tonight. We are very sorry to leave behind our very good friends here, especially the Vicar, and we do hope that when we are back in England, members of St Andrew's Church will pay us a visit when they return home.

"We have a very great affection for the Church for we were married here 18 years ago and our first daughter was baptised in this Church."

Members of the congregation of St Andrew's Church last night held a farewell party for Mr and Mrs G. S. P. Heywood. Mr Heywood is the retiring Director of the Royal Observatory. During the function, the Rev. J. H. Ogilvie (left) presented a Bible and a pipe to Mr Heywood and a brooch to Mrs Heywood.—(Staff Photographer).

Tributes to Mr Heywood

A TRIBUTE TO MR. HEYWOOD

The funeral took place at Lockerley on Tuesday of Mr. Graham Heywood. A Scouting colleague writes: "Graham Heywood was a quite exceptional man and the Scouts of Lockerley, Romsey and Hampshire were privileged to share his company.

Mr. Graham Heywood as many in the Scouting Movement will remember him

"His Scouting history has been well told in the *Advertiser* of last week, but his friends who were Scouting with him over many years will want to pay tribute to his modesty, his leadership and to his overwhelming kindness and generosity of spirit.

"Nothing was too much trouble—no loyalty was too trivial to be honoured. He never said, or thought, I am sure, an unkind word. All our recollections of him will bear out, and more, the stories that we heard of his life in the internment camps, where he gave example, comfort and leadership to many: far, far, above the gift of an ordinary man."

DEATH OF SCOUTING VETERAN

The death occurred on Wednesday of Mr. Graham Heywood, Critchells, Lockerley, who in 1969 received the Silver Acorn, one of Scouting's top awards, at a time when he was an Assistant County Commissioner.

Although as a Boy Scout he remembered that his good deed for the day was weeding his headmaster's garden it was not until 1929 that he became a Group Scoutmaster at Burford Oxfordshire, to continue an association with Scouting at home and abroad including Hong Kong which was to last for the rest of his life.

In the Far East Mr. Heywood was sent with a colleague to retrieve valuable equipment but was taken prisoner in 1941 by the advancing Japanese. During his imprisonment in Shum Shi Po camp in Hong Kong he kept a diary on fragments of paper. He was released by the Allied Victory and returned to Hong Kong in 1946 as Director of The Royal Observatory.

There followed a period of re-establishment of the observatory despite acute shortages of staff and equipment.

He retired in 1955 and shortly after settled at Critchells, Lockerley. A man with his long experience in Scouting was soon busy again. He was appointed Senior Scout Leader with the 24th Romsey (Embley Park School) until November 1957 when he reformed the 6th Romsey (Lockerley). He was appointed as Assistant County Commissioner (Leader Training) in 1960.

When the award was made in 1969 the then District Commissioner, Mr. David Plunkett, said that Mr. Heywood had given a lifetime of service both in this country and abroad. The editor of Woodsmoke said: "that in Graham Heywood Lockerley village has enjoyed the devotion of a true Scouter and Churchwarden."

The funeral service for Mr. Heywood, who is survived by his wife, Mrs. Valerie Heywood, takes place at St. John's, Lockerley, next week.

Graham Scudamore Percival Heywood (E 1917-22), o. son of Col. G. G. P. Heywood (C 1880) and Mary, d. of Ven. the Hon. B. L. S. Stanhope, Archdeacon of Hereford. New Coll., Oxon. 1922, 2 Nat. Sci. 1925, B.Sc. 1926, M.A. 1933; O.U. Shooting VIII; cox of New Coll. VIII, 1926; researched into properties of Electricity; taught briefly at Radley; Research Asst. Leafield Meterolog. station 1928; signed on as Meteorologist to Antarctic Expedi. which was cancelled in the depression; asst. R. Observatory, Hong Kong 1932; while in Hong Kong pursued many interests, rowing, sailing, singing, climbing (a life-long interest inspired by his Housedon R.L.G.I.), flower-hunting with a botanist friend, and bird-watching — and spent a leave on the Trans-Siberian Rly. In June 1937 married Valerie Rose Isobel (Railton Wyatt) and they had two daughters and four grandchildren. A gunner in the H.K.V.D.F. in 1941, was a P.O.W. 1941-45, but after recuperating in England returned to Hong Kong to be Dir. of R. Observatory there, 1946-55. Experienced several typhoons during term of office, but collected valuable data both for growing air traffic, and for N.A.S.A.'s early space researches. A member of the Alpine Club, climbed many summits in Snowdonia, Ireland and the Alps, and aged 79 reached the top of Caradoc in Church Stretton. When he retired from Hong Kong, returned to Shropshire, but soon sold the family home in Much Wenlock and made his home at Lockerley, near Romsey. There he soon became immersed in village affairs and Hampshire Scouting. In 1969 received the Silver Acorn, while he was an assistant County Commissioner and Training Leader. A Church Warden for many years, on the P.C.C., worked for the school, and was Sec. of the Village Hall. Author of *The Upper Winds of Hong Kong* and *Rambles in Hong Kong* and a number of Scientific papers. F.R. Meterolog. Soc. A great family man, gardener, bell-ringer, and took up painting and kept up the carpentry he had learnt from Win. Coll. Died peacefully at his home 23rd January, 1985.

From *Romsey Advertiser* (Romsey is about 8 km southeast of Lockerley)

From a Scouting colleague

From *Wykehamist* (Winchester College magazine)

Lockerley Parish News Letter March 1985

With the recent death of Mr Graham Heywood we have certainly lost someone from the local community who packed the thirty or so years of his retirement in Lockerley with effort to benefit the village and a wider circle. As I said at his funeral, it would be right to describe Graham with the same words used of St. Barnabas, as 'A good man , full of the holy spirit and of faith'. Whatever he did he did with vigour, meticulous attention to detail, grace and humility; whether it was for the Church, where he was Churchwarden for many years, or for the Parish Council, the School, the Village Hall which he served as Secretary also for a very long time, for many other local clubs, associations an activities, and for the scouts where perhaps he will be remembered with most affection for re-forming the Lockerley Scout Group and leading it and training other leaders in the locality.

Graham's life spanned 82 years, and from his home in Shropshire, he moved to school at Winchester, University at Oxford , a career in Meteorology in Hongkong and in the midst of which he married Valerie, and soon after underwent great suffering in a prisoner of war camp near Hongkong for four years; mercifully Valerie and their daughter Susan managed to be evacuated to Australia where Veronica was born.

Retirement in 1955 eventually led to living at Critchells, Lockerley. All this time Graham had been a keen scouter and also a mountaineer; music was another of his interests. Everyone who has had the privilege of working with Graham holds him in great esteem and respect, he could be described as a true Christian gentleman, whose example and inspiration must sustain us all in any effort we make to contribute to the service of God and our fellows. Adored by his wife and family, Graham was a true family man; his life of pilgrimage did involve some extreme suffering, he showed great moral, spiritual and physical courage, and he showed his love for others in very practical and sensible ways. At the service we sang 'Who would true valour see, let him come hither' Who would true valour see? I echo, let him be taught by Graham Heywood. May God Bless and watch over Valerie and all the family.

From the Lockerley Parish

Editor's note

As a historian and teacher, I have read countless books, diaries and accounts of experiences written by prisoners of war, including civilian internees. I have also heard many stories told by such people. When I first read Mr Heywood's account of his experiences during World War II in Hong Kong and in particular his experiences in Shamshuipo military POW camp, I was astounded. Never had I read or heard such a remarkable account, being so sincere, inspiring and optimistic.

I was delighted to be asked to help with the editing of this book, because it led to my meeting and getting to know Mr Heywood's daughter, Veronica, when she visited Hong Kong in 2013. Together with her and the present Director of the Hong Kong Observatory, Mr Shun Chi Ming, we visited Au Tau village in the New Territories, Hong Kong, where Mr Heywood had been captured by the Japanese on 8th December 1941. Talk about history coming to life!

I would like to pay tribute here to Chi Ming for liaising with the Heywood family in England to obtain information about Mr Heywood's life as well as many of the illustrations in the book. Chi Ming's interest in and enthusiasm for the history of the Hong Kong Observatory is indeed most commendable and deserving of the highest praise.

The part I have played as Editor is in reality a very small one compared to the roles of the Heywood family and Chi Ming. Nevertheless, I am very pleased to have played a role, however small. Some 50+ years ago,

I participated in an oratorical contest in upstate New York, USA, as a high school student. At that time I came across a quotation which has remained with me over the years and came to mind when I began to write about my role as Editor. The quotation is, "Even to be so small a part of so great a thing is greatness". This book is a great book and will certainly be an inspiration to all its readers.

G C Emerson

May 2015

THE DIARY

CHAPTER I

CAPTURE

"No one out here minds a war more or less, but travelling in the opposite direction to an advancing army is apt to cause discomfort and delay" – Vare

The air-raid alarm interrupted my shave on that Monday morning, December 8th, 1941. As I clattered downstairs and hurried along the path from my quarters to my office, my first feelings were almost of relief; so the Japs had come at last, and the years of threats and crises were over.

We were all ready for air raids at the Observatory. The underground Seismograph Room made an admirable shelter, our carefully rehearsed air-raid drill went smoothly, and within a few minutes of the sounding of the sirens were assembled in the basement. More too soon, for Jap planes were already over Hong Kong, dive-bombing the airport.

The roll was called; all present. The European staff consisted of B.D. Evans, Director of the Observatory, with myself and Leonard Starbuck as his assistants. The rest were Chinese ... computors on duty, office coolies and household servants ... who had filed in and now stood around the room with self-conscious grins on their friendly faces.

The Royal Observatory in the 1930s

Hoisting No.1 Typhoon signal at the Observatory –
Heywood is second from the right

"It's a very good practice raid, isn't it, sir!" said one of the computors to me, as the racket of A.A. fire and falling bombs came faintly to us down the staircase. I had to tell him that I was afraid it was the real thing.

The raid over, I returned to my breakfast, little thinking that it was the last really civilized meal I should eat for years. I was alone, except for Mike, our cocker spaniel. My wife and daughter had been evacuated to Australia in 1940, and my messmate, another Government servant who was sharing my quarters, had already been mobilised with the Hong Kong Volunteers.

Group photo of the Observatory's staff in 1932 (centre of front row: Mr
Benjamin D Evans, Mr Charles W Jeffries and Mr Heywood). Mr Jeffries
was Director of the Observatory until he died of a stroke in June 1941. He is
buried in Hong Kong Cemetery, Happy Valley.

Hong Kong is at its best in early winter, and it was a lovely morning,
clear and fresh, with a few light clouds drifting across the sky. The garden
and surrounding wood looked cool and green, and through the pine-
trees I could see glimpses of the harbour sparkling in the vivid sunshine
and lively with craft of all sizes. Beyond lay the city of Hong Kong, the
white buildings crowding the waterfront and thinning out behind the
trees on the lower slopes of the island. Behind the city the hills rose
steeply, culminating in the familiar sky-line of Victoria Peak. We used
to boast that Hong Kong harbour was the loveliest in the world. The
Observatory and its adjoining quarters stood on a low wooded hill in
Kowloon, a rapidly growing town on the mainland facing Hong Kong
Island. It was a pleasant place, Observatory Hill, and I had grown very
fond of it, for it had been my home for nearly ten years. Returning to the
office after breakfast, I found Evans in his room studying an important-
looking file marked "secret", which he had just taken out of the safe. It

contained our emergency instructions. The first item on the programme was to dismantle our magnetic station at Au Tau, and bring in all the instruments and equipment to safety. Au Tau was out in the country, near the border of British territory, some 25 miles from Kowloon by road. It was decided that Starbuck should go out with a lorry to do this job, leaving Evans and myself to carry on with the ordinary routine work of issuing the morning weather forecasts, time-signals and so on.

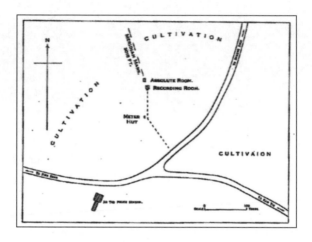

Layout of Au Tau Magnetic Station (see map on page 8-9)

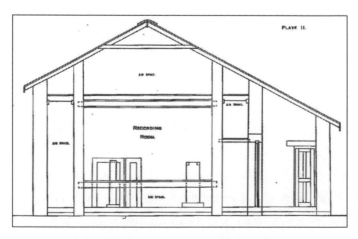

Recording room of Au Tau Magnetic Station

But a lorry could not be obtained. Two smaller cars would be needed to bring in all the gear, and eventually we arranged that both Starbuck and myself should go out, driving two private cars.

So I told Ah Bing, my Chinese cook, to pack some sandwiches, and Leonard and I started off about 11 a.m. armed with tool-kit, picnic lunches and incongruous tin hats. It never entered our heads that we should not return that evening, and I have been kicking myself ever since that I failed to provide for our faithful household staff, or for Mike. I hope that the servants helped themselves to the small hoard of tinned goods in the larder.

Leonard Starbuck

So we trundled down the drive and away through the streets of Kowloon, which were buzzing with excitement as the outbreak of war. Out in the country we passed some small detachments of troops,... a picket of Royal Scots at a barbed wire barrier, a party of R.E.'s standing by to blow up a bridge, and a Volunteer armoured car on advanced patrol. They looked at our pass and let us through; when asked whether we should find any difficulty in returning that afternoon, they replied "Oh, no, you'll be all right: if there's any trouble you'll hear firing on the border, and there'll be plenty of time for you to get back."

We reached our destination at noon, to find the place deserted; the Chinese caretaker had beat it (in which he showed more foresight than we), but we had brought our own keys, and were soon at work dismantling the instruments. We knocked off at 1 p.m. and sat eating our lunch on a grassy knoll among the pine-trees, with the sunshine warm on our backs. All was quiet and peaceful, and as we looked across the Shum Chun estuary into Chinese territory a few miles away, it was difficult to realise that Japanese troops might be massing there to invade the Colony. But we were soon reminded that the war had started, for while we were lunching

Heywood's quarters and his household staff (Ah Bing on the extreme right)
photographed before the war.

a formation of Japanese planes (about 20) passed over on their way to bomb Hong Kong. We returned to work in the hut: if we had had any sense, one of us would have remained outside to watch the approaches, but there had been no sound of firing, so it was obvious, we thought, that no Japs could be near. We were far too light-hearted about it all.

By about 3 p.m. we had finished our task. Len had disappeared round a corner of the path with an armful of instruments for the cars, which were standing at the roadside some 200 yards from the hut. I was standing in my shirtsleeves, keeping an eye on the pile of paraphanalia until he should reappear. It struck me that he was away for rather a long time, so I strolled to the corner to see what had happened to him. There he was, standing with his hands up and a most disgusted expression on his face, while two Jap soldiers in full battle kit searched him. For a wild moment I wondered whether to make bolt for it: I didn't like the idea of deserting Len, and while I hesitated the Japs spotted me, so I reluctantly joined the party. We were soon squatting side by side, tied to a tree on the steep hillside overlooking Au Tau police station.

That morning I had enjoyed a tasty breakfast under my own roof, in the afternoon I was a captive in the hands of the Japanese; it was certainly a rude and sudden change, and we thought it likely that we had the unenviable distinction of being the very first prisoners to be taken in the war of East Asia. But at first we could hardly take in all the unpleasant implications of the situation and our feelings were rather of excitement and amusement than of dismay. It all seemed so incredible and theatrical, it couldn't really be we who were captured in a blitz .... Such things just didn't happen to law-abiding civil servants in a respectable British colony. It was not until the next day that our adventure began to seem a grim one.

Our Guards were kindly disposed, giving us a drink of water and a packet of cigarettes, the latter ironically labeled "Homeward Bound". They appeared to be an advanced patrol, for they busied themselves setting up a machine gun, and grinding away at a portable radio transmitter, while their two officers studied maps. Bye and bye more troops arrived in lorries and began to occupy the police station. The junior of the two officers spoke a little English, for he had been educated at a university, and appeared to be a young man of some culture and refinement; he questioned us at length … the first of many interrogations that we were to undergo. We must have appeared suspicious characters … found in mufti in enemy territory. Were we spies? Or had we been concerned in the blowing up of a road bridge nearby? We had great difficulty in explaining ourselves, but at last the two officers seemed satisfied.

At dusk we were untied and taken down to the police station where we were allowed to do a little looting on our own account. Additional clothes were welcome, for I had been taken in my shirt-sleeves and was not allowed to retrieve my coat. Providentially my pipe and tobacco-pouch were in my trouser pocket; these, with the clothes I stood up in, were my only possessions. I secured a coat, many sizes too large for me, and a towel. We also helped ourselves to an unappetising meal of cold rice, butter and jam.

Japanese troops advancing in the New Territories *[3]*

Outside on the grass the troops were cooking their evening meal; the little fires winked in the darkness, revealing the shadowy forms of horses tethered to trees in the background. The column now assembled amounted to perhaps a battalion, with numerous pack-horses, but no mechanical transport. After a while we were marched off with the troops along the road leading to the unfinished airfield a Kam Tin; an affable soldier next to me insisted on walking with his arm around my neck … was it affection or detention? Probably the latter, though I was reminded of an evening stroll down a country lane in Japan, arm in arm with two slightly tipsy gentlemen who were trying to point out to me the beauties of Fuji in the darkness.

The tramp of tired boots under heavy packs made me think of Churchill's remark about the German hordes, with no liberties of their own, yet always trampling on the liberties of others. The column halted near the airfield; tired out, we lay down on the hard concrete road and slept fitfully. I thought of Evans, and how worried he must be at our failure to return. And what would happen to all our belongings, and our servants, and Mike? "Missing, believed captured" … and would word reach our families that we were safe?

All armies, the Japanese included, seem apt to follow the Duke of York's tactics, for in the middle of the night we fell in and marched back again by the way we had come. Finally we turned off the hills to the south. The inhabitants had fled; doors were broken open, and grass was spread in the yard in front of the houses. There we slept, huddled among the troops.

It was day when we awoke; the friendliness of the previous evening had evaporated; the officers were un-communicative, and nobody seemed inclined to give us any breakfast. At last someone tossed us a few biscuits, which we munched dismally. The officers were obviously conferring about us, and finally detailed a squad of six armed men to lead us off; it was a nasty moment … was this a firing party? But no, we were taken a couple of miles across country to a fair-sized house on the outskirts of a village. This appeared to be a battalion head-quarters judging by the number of field-telephones' wires radiating from it, and by an air of bustle and activity. An air-raid was in progress over Hong Kong, and a soldier joyfully showed me a leaflet luridly depicting the destruction of my home town. I think my spirits touched rock-bottom at that moment, but I was somewhat cheered when we managed to secure a small dish of meat and a sip of water.

Kowloon under air raid in 1941, showing Sacred Hill (see also photos [18] and [19]) to the right of the bombing, Kai Tak airport and the three-storey residential buildings of "Kai Tak Bund" between Sacred Hill and the airport [4]

An officer came out of the house and gave instructions to another squad, pointing to us and making significant gestures with his hands about his throat. As we were lad off, we looked apprehensively around for ropes, and convenient trees with low branches, but it turned out that we were merely to join a party of stretcher-bearers and coolies. We were given a pole and a load between us to which our unfeeling guards added heavy bits of equipment from time to time. A thin rain had begun to fall, and we had a horrible march across country, urged on by the rifle-butts of our guards. We begun to wonder of we should loss our identities and become coolies in the Japanese army for the rest of the war. We passed a number of troops on the path; we were used to being stared at by now, but we did not like a mounted officer who said rude things about us, with a look of hatred on his face ... it seemed uncalled-for.

We passed Fanling golf course ... its greens forlorn with broken bottles and overturned rickshaws ... and finally halted at Sheung Shui, where we sat down dejectedly on the road, and felt that we were nobody's babies. Later three guards took us on foot and by lorry to Tai Po, a large village some 15 miles by road from Kowloon. We noticed that, although it was only the second day of the invasion, and enormous road demolition had already been made good for traffic. We reached Tai Po after dark and were led to the G.H.Q., a row of large Chinese houses over-looking the wrecked railway bridge.

One of these houses was occupied by the Intelligence section, and here we underwent another inquisition, this time by interpreters with a fair knowledge of English. Hitherto we had been questioned together, and Len had done most of the answering, speaking very slowly and emphatically in his best pidgin English, while I had only chipped in occasionally. But now we were summoned into the room one by one. Fortunately, the partition was thin, and each of us could hear everything the other said, so we were able to spin a consistent yarn. This was necessary, for we did not wish to disclose any of the war-time activities of the Observatory. As for military dispositions in Hong Kong, it was soon obvious that our questioners knew a lot more about them than we did. They were very suspicious at first, but finally we managed to persuade them that we were harmless scientists. The leading interpreter, a Mr. Mianti, was a villanouslooking fellow with one eye; he turned out later to be a University lecturer and quite a friendly individual.

They gave us supper … our first square meal since yesterday's breakfast. Feeling somewhat revived, we were taken to a squalid little room in the coolie quarters. Immediately outside the door was the closet; its drain, as is usual in the back regions of Chinese houses, was blocked, and the little yard was half flooded. Some miserable half-fledged chicks were dying of dampness and starvation. We were too weary to bother about the smell, and were soon asleep.

The following morning we felt we were going to go up in the social scale, for we were taken to see the General next door. He was a cheerful, tubby little man, dressed in tunic, breeches and white open-necked shirt. He waved us affably into chairs, and talked to us through an interpreter, while we sat sipping tea and smoking.

After a few questions, he suddenly said "If I set you free, where would you like to go?"

When we had recovered from our astonishment, we replied that we would like to return to Hong Kong.

"Why?"

"We want to join our friends."

"Very sorry; you cannot go through the fighting; it would be too dangerous. But soon Hong Kong will fall, then we send you back to England." … presumably when the war was over and the Far East cleared of Europeans.

Like all the Japs to whom we spoke, he was completely confident that the fall of Hong Kong would not be long-delayed, and we were bound to admit that he had good reason. He was obviously anxious that we should think well of the Japanese forces; we could truthfully say we had seen no cruelty, and had been treated on the whole with some consideration.

That evening, December 10th, British and Indian prisoners from a captured pill-box at Shing Mun redoubt began to arrive, weary, disheveled and disheartened; we were not allowed to communicate with them. They underwent a much more searching interrogation than we. The Indian soldiers were questioned by two particularly smug and unpleasant Indian interpreters; one of these, as we learned subsequently, had been connected with a military outfitting firm in Hong Kong. We admired one Indian N.C.O., who for half the night was subjected to intensive anti-British propaganda, but refused to budge an inch in his allegiance.

Next day we managed to get a little fresh air and exercise in a narrow yard at the side of the house; a heavy battery was firing at regular intervals somewhere near. In the evening Mianti and his fellow-interpreters burst into our little room shouting "Kowloon is freed". Oozing with affability, they sat on our bed and celebrated the occasion with a bottle of saki, which they wished us to share. I felt far from festive; now, I reflected the yellow blight which had been spreading for years over the Far East had settled on Kowloon; it too would be brought to misery and starvation, like so many other places in the "Co-Prosperity Sphere". We had made friends with the Japanese quarter-master and cook, a cherubic young conscript, whose large glasses and moon-like face gave him a most unwarlike appearance. He shared our view that the whole business of war was absurd, and seemed quite unmoved by the news of victory.

We did not have long to cultivate this new acquaintance, however, for the following afternoon all the prisoners were packed into a lorry at a moment's notice, and whisked away to a new place of captivity. The cook, looking less martial than ever, waved us an almost tearful farewell.

Chapter 2

The Gilded Cage

"If you have never been under restraint before and never known what is was to be a captive, you feel a sense of constant humiliation in being confined in a narrow space, fenced in by railings and wire, watched by armed men" – Winston Churchill

The lorry took us to a beautiful Chinese-style house which had been built near Fanling by a rich American. It stood on a little wooded hill, and looked out over the paddy-fields to the mountains over which I used to walk. The buildings, roofed with blue glazed tiles, were grouped round two shady courtyards. The commandant of the prison occupied the upper part of the main building, while the three British officers were put into a comfortable room below him. Len and I, mere civilians, were herded with the remainder of the prisoners, sixty in all, into the hall between the courtyards. There were about twenty Royal Scots from Shing Mun, a solitary Canadian who had lost his way in Kowloon, and the rest were Indians. We gathered later that we were the only prisoners taken on the mainland.

The hall was furnished with a handsome carved table and a few chairs. We were given rush mats, blankets and a meager supply of toilet necessities. The catering arrangements consisted of a number of bags of flour and a charcoal brazier … that was all. Supper presented rather a

Prisoners of war captured in the New Territories in 1941 *[5]*

problem; fortunately for us, the faithful Chinese amah had stuck to her post during the invasion, although advised to flee by the police. This excellent old lady came to our rescue with firewood, cooking utencils, peanut oil, and an exquisite porcelain dinner-service. We were soon frying pancakes over a cheerful fire in the open hearth.

During the first days of our stay at Sheung Shui we were very strictly confined. We were allowed out of the hall only for visits to the latrine, in charge of a sentry, and for ten minutes' P.T. morning and evening in the courtyard under a genial Jap N.C.O. The room was overcrowded, the habits of some of our fellow captives unpleasant, flies swarmed on hot days. The two wounded men who were with us had a bad time for the first few days, for they received no proper attention, and could not even change their clothes. Capt. J......, the senior British officer, did not appear for nearly a week; finally, to our amusement, he burst into our room with a great show of concern, saying "Where are my wounded men? I must see my wounded!"

After a while, the British prisoners were moved into the library, leaving the Indians in the hall. This was a great improvement, for though there was still only just enough room for us to sleep on the floor, we had the rum of well-stocked bookshelves. Also we were gradually allowed more freedom; we could sit in the courtroom whenever we liked, and once a day we walked and sunned ourselves on the terrace outside. Sometimes we were even permitted to go down to the little river at the foot of the garden to wash our clothes and bathe.

We soon settled down amicably with our fellow-captives, who put up politely with our public-school accents. There was plenty to talk about, and Len, who is a more sociable being than I, made up for my deficiencies in this respect.

It was a lazy life; the only job requiring any hard work was the carrying up of tins of water from the river. The water was brown with mud, and had to be boiled for drinking. The Japs are partial to hot baths, and many gallons had to be carried up every day to fill a big tub, which they rigged up over an open fire-place. We were sometimes privileged to watch one of our captors simmering gently in his hot tub, with a fire crackling underneath and only his head appearing at the top, surrounded by clouds of steam.

Of course we groused about the food, but it was adequate. Rice and pancakes formed the foundation; these were supplemented by vegetables, and occasionally, when the guards had killed a pig, by a little pork. Once we were feasted on whale-meat, which I believe is consumed in large quantities in Japan; the Indians thought it was beef, so we had their share.

On Christmas Day the sounds of warfare ceased in the south, and we knew that Hong Kong had fallen. Ever since our first contact with the Japanese forces this had seemed to us almost inevitable, and now we could only feel thankful that the bloody business was over. For just a hundred years Hong Kong had been a British Colony; in that period it had developed from a barren island inhabited by a few fishing people to one of the greatest ports in the world, with a population of over a million.

Maybe there were things of which we were not proud in the Colony, but at least it had been a place where thousands of Chinese had found a livelihood and security and fair-dealing. And now the last refuge of the oppressed in the whole of China had fallen under the blight.

Victory parade of Japanese troops in Wanchai, Hong Kong Island, 28 December 1941 [6]

We watched a huge column of smoke towering up into the sky to the southward; it drifted over us in the upper arc, dimming the sun, and we wondered whether it came from the whole of the city being on fire. Later we learned that it had come from the burning oil depot at North Point, which had been fired when the Japanese landed on the Island.

It was a queer Christmas Day. I persuaded a sentry to escort me down to the stream for a bathe, which cheered me up somewhat, and in the evening Len and I were invited with the officers to a jollification in the Commandant's room. Those of the guard who were off duty were summoned, and sat down sheepishly, with their mouths open and their hands on their knees. The saki bottle circulated freely, and the Japs became very amicable. They sang their favourite choruses, we replied with ours, and the Commandant, a kindly middle-aged nonentity with a taste for music, beamed on us through his glasses from the head of the table. Capt. J...... obliged with a song in a booming bass voice; his black beard was coming on nicely, and a woman's fur coat, flung over his shoulders, gave him a rakish appearance. The star turn of the evening, however, was given by one of the Japs, who, when called upon to perform, stood up and sang "Where is my wandering boy tonight?"

Len and I ate as much food as we could with decency and furtively stuffed our pockets with cigarettes for our friends down below, who had not been invited.

Japanese victory parade in Causeway Bay, Hong Kong Island, 28 December 1941 *[7]*

The days passed slowly. The weather was brilliantly fine, and it was pleasant to sit in the sun on the terrace, tracing routes up the well-remembered hills, or watching the country-people at work in the fields, I used to plot escapes with Wilcox, a young Artillery officer. I was not supposed to communicate with the officers, so our conferences had to be a little conspiratorial. We should probably have had little difficulty in getting away to the hills, but the further outlook was discouraging, for we had no money, no reserve food and insufficient clothing. Nor did we know what punishments the Japs were likely to inflict on recaptured prisoners; as likely as not we should be shot or beheaded, and altogether the enterprise did not seem a suitable one for a married man.

On January 8th, just a month after our capture, we were roused before dawn, and told that we should be shifted to Hong Kong. The troops were jubilant, thinking that any change would be for the better, but I had my doubts. I had great hopes of smuggling away a volume or two of the Encyclopedia Britannica for future reading, but unfortunately no books were allowed to be taken. After interminable delays all the prisoners were packed into two lorries and started for town. We avoided the shorter route via Tai Po, presumably because it was blocked by the pathetic stream of Chinese refugees trekking inland from Hong Kong. This "repatriation", as the Japanese called it, continued for many days, and hundreds of thousands of people must have left the Colony.

The lorries took the Castle Peak road, and as we passed Fanling we noticed the swastika flying over a large house, which may have been the headquarters of the German advisers to the Japanese invasion forces. Certainly the tremendous swiftness and drive of all the Japanese offensives at the outbreak of war strongly suggested German influence.

The fine weather still held, and the hills stood up clear and hard against a pale blue sky. The road ran first through the paddy-growing country around Yuen Long, then would in and out of the bays and headlands of the lovely coast between Castle Peak and Kowloon. A beautiful drive, but it depressed me to see the New Territories in the hands of the invader. When we topped the rise of Lai Chi Kok hill, however, and saw Hong Kong once more, I was glad to see that the city had apparently suffered little damage. Judging from the noise we had heard, I had expected to find it laid flat, but the Jap bombing and shelling had been confined on the whole to military objectives.

On reaching the outskirts of Kowloon, we turned off the mainroad and drew up at the gates of Sham Shui Po[5] camp, which was to be my abode for the next three years.

---

5 "Sham Shui Po" is used throughout the book for consistency with current usage, even though "Shum Shui Po" was often used at the time.

CHAPTER 3

SHAM SHUI PO

"It's hard to be wise on an empty stomach" – George Eliot

Sham Shui Po Camp c.1930 *[8]*

Len and I had hopes of being sent to the civilian internment camp at Stanley, on the south side of Hong Kong Island, where all the British non-combatants were confined. In spite of our protests, however, the Japs throughout treated us as prisoners of war, and on arrival at Sham Shui Po we were dumped in the middle of the road with the other prisoners. The officers were detailed off to their quarters, the Royal Scots to their lines, the Canadian to his; the Indians were conducted to the far corner of the camp, and we two were left standing in the road with "no home, no momma, no poppa, no chow", as the little Chinese beggar-boys say.

Formerly we had both been members of the Hong Kong Volunteers, until it was decided that our whole-time service would be required by the Observatory in war-time we therefore sought them out, and after much palaver were finally attached to one of the volunteer companies.

We must have looked a disreputable pair. We were both perforce growing beards, which had not as yet attained a dignified brushiness, and we wanted a haircut. As the weather was chilly, Len was wearing an ancient Chinese padded coat, which had once been a gay canary-yellow, while I had the Police Officer's best dark pin-stripe coat, reefed in by an old puttee around my waist. Our own shoes and grey flannel trousers, all due for cleaning, completed the rig-out. We had no luggage.

We did not feel lonely, for innumerable friends looked us up and greeted us as though we had returned from the dead. I was almost overwhelmed with gratitude when a number of my old Rover Scouts insisted on making up my kit out of their own slender stocks; one gave me a pair of slacks, another some underclothing, another a piece of soap and a large tin of tobacco … for which my soul was crying out. These gifts represented a real sacrifice, for my friends only had what they had been able to carry with them when they came over from Hong Kong. It was a case of the widow's mite, and I shall never be able to repay them adequately.

A comic verse, *The P.O.W. Rover*, written by Heywood:

In Shum Shui Po, in Shum Shui Po,

Your life may seem a trifle slow,

But if you join our Rover Crew

You'll find no end of things to do;

The doleful dumps will cease to trouble you,

Although you are a P.O.W.

Publicity we do not seek,

And furtively we meet each week,

Because you see the Japanese

Have banned all meetings such as these,

And we have no intense desire
To rouse Slap Happy's vengeful ire.

There's not much chance to go a hike;
Or sail a boat, or ride a bike;
Should you be found with Bergen pack
Bulging with camp gear on your back,
Misunderstandings might arise
Resulting in your swift demise.

Still, never mind, there ain't no sense
In planning jaunts outside the fence,
When you can exercise your brains
On any subject that remains
In P.O.R. (a publication
stuffed full of priceless information).

If Pioneering is your hobby
You'll get some useful hints from Robbie;
The Skipper talks about the stars,
And whether there be Scouts on Mars;
While if you want to learn 1st Aid,
Bill is your lecturer (unpaid).
The Rover Mates are all live wires;
At cooking Dunlop never tires,
While Curley cares for ailing chaps,
And Crab looks after pipes and taps.
But once their daily task is over
They rush to coach the budding Rover,
And rouse in each recruit a zest
To pass the fearsome Red Stripe Test.

To pass the fearsome Red Stripe Test.

Now when our serious work is done
We turn to frolic and to fun,
And if the crew bursts into song
You'll hear the Padre going strong.
We may, if it is not too late,
Indulge in quizzes or debate,
Or maybe for a special lark
Organise wild games in the dark
(But don't, like Bill, attempt to nab
A sentry, or you'll get a jab).

"Gee whizz! Lights out! We must pack up!
You haven't served me with a cup
Of cocoa, or a festive bun;
In my last crew 'twas ALWAYS done!"
"Such luxuries, my lad, must wait
Until the day when through the gate
With happy hearts away we go
From Shum Shui Po, from Shum Shui Po."

But my delight at finding so many friends was tempered when I learned of the casualties. The eighteen days' defence of Hong Kong had cost us dear, and as usual it seemed that the best men had been the first to be taken. Was it worth it, I wonder? Many of my friends had gone, and of a rollicking party of four who had gone on a walking tour together last Chinese New Year's holiday, I was the only survivor.

Sham Shui Po was a military camp standing on reclaimed ground between the sea and the northern outskirts of Kowloon. Like a Roman Camp, it was intersected by two wide roads, crossing one another at right angles in the centre. The main road was flanked on either side by grass plots, fronting small huts which had been used as offices, orderly rooms and so on. Behind these were the Lines, row upon row of long, low barrack huts, of a depressing uniformity. Behind the lines were the kitchens and wash-houses, and beyond the latter, alongside the fence, were the latrines. On the south side of the cross-roads were the sergeants' mess, former NAAFO buildings, etc., and the main road at each and opened out into a spacious parade ground of beaten earth, which reflected a dazzling glare on sunny days. Along the sea wall on the far side of the parade ground was a huge and hideous block of flats, known as Jubilee Buildings; these had been the married quarters.

The camp had been long condemned, and was due for demolition as soon as more up-to-date barracks had been built. The troops stationed

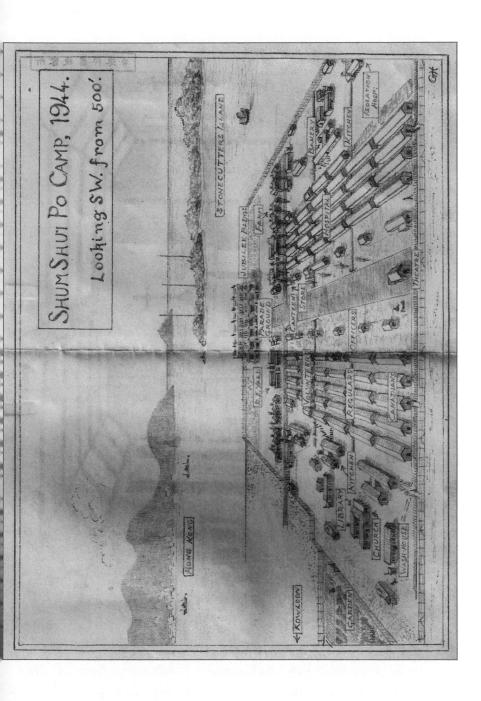

Above: The Sham Shui Po camp taken from the north, with the Jubilee
Buildings on the right in the middle facing the harbour (c.1946-47) *[9]*.
Facing page: Sketch by Heywood: "Where are those blue, remembered hills?"
on a piece of paper from the POW camp labelled in Chinese meaning "Hong
Kong Prisoners of War Internment Camp".

there used to curse it heartily; it was too hot in summer, too cold in winter;
it was uncomfortable; and the sanitary arrangements were primitive. But
it had been a paradise compared to its present state, for during the war
the whole place had been thoroughly looted by the Chinese. When we
arrived, not a single window was left in any of the huts; doors, shelves,
electric-light fittings had all gone; not a stick of furniture remained
except a number of ancient army iron beds, and most of the taps had
disappeared from the wash-houses. To add to the desolation, the camp
had been bombed; several huts were in ruins, and there was a large hole in
the corner of Jubilee Buildings. When the weather was cold and cloudy
it would be difficult to imagine anywhere more dreary than the camp
during the early days of our occupation.

It had, however, certain advantages as a P.O.W. camp; there was any
amount of room within the barbed wire fence, and sometimes one would

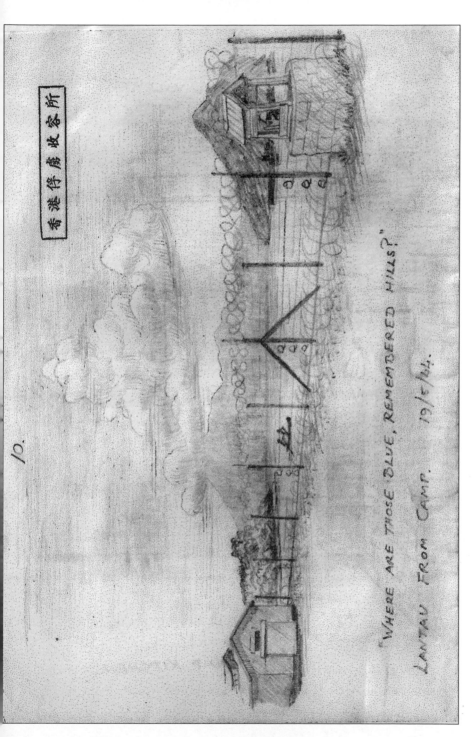

10.

"WHERE ARE THOSE BLUE, REMEMBERED HILLS?"

LANTAU FROM CAMP. 19/5/44.

香港俘虜收容所

hardly see a Jap all day. In this respect it was a great improvement on Sheung Shui, where our captors used to drop in to watch us eating, as though we were monkeys in a cage. Also it was a great relief not to have to fetch all our water in buckets from a dirty stream. In Sham Shui Po we were at least well off for fresh air and cold water. And the outlook was good; the hills stood around the camp to the north, and on the seaward side we looked across the water to the islands of Hong Kong, Stonecutters and Lantau. On clear days I could plainly see the Observatory, and the roof of my quarters showing above the trees; a strange fate to be cooped up as a P.O.W. within sight of my home! The boat-builders yard where I used to keep my sailing dingy was within a few hundred yards of the camp. I could see the headland on Stonecutters where my wife and I had once run ashore, the awkward tide-race where we had once rescued the occupants of two capsized sailing-canoes; the shining stretch of water over which we had gaily sailed away for a week-end camp on Lantau. Yes, you could spend a lot of time in Sham Shui Po re-living the past, but on the whole if was as well not to, for you were apt to become depressed; better to live for each day as it came along, and make the best of the present.

The company to which we were attached occupied the Theatre, a large draughty hut at the northern end of the main road. Fortunately it had a wooden floor, which was slightly less cold and hard to sleep on than the usual concrete. My new companions provided my blanket and greatcoat. These, by the way, had been humped along on the weary "Victory March" after the surrender, when the prisoners had carried all their gear some three or four miles through the streets of Kowloon on the way from the ferry to the camp. I was glad of the loan, for it was bitterly cold at night, and never was the sun more welcome in the mornings.

There was a fortnight of unutterable discomfort in February, when the sun never shone at all, and an unrelenting north wind whiffled through the huts. You feel the cold when you are on short commons; during these days it was almost impossible to achieve the smallest sense of physical comfort at any hour of the twenty-four, and only the hardiest braved the cold showers. What must it be like to be a P.O.W. in a really cold climate!

We were hungry! When we first arrived in Sham Shui Po our daily ration consisted of two meals of boiled rice, with water to drink .... nothing more. The cooks had not yet learned the art of producing light flaky rice in bulk, and the rations were often soggy or burnt. Most of my companions eked out their meals with tinned food which they had brought with them. There was also a brisk trade in foodstuffs over the wire every day. A crowd of all ranks, from colonels to privates, jostled against the fence, bidding for packets of sugar and looted tinned goods from Chinese children who had run the gauntlet of the sentries. I was completely penniless, so these luxuries were not for me. As I ate my meager portion of rice, my mouth used to water at the sight of my neighbours tucking in to bully-beef and biscuits. Hunger is very depressing; the next meal seems horribly remote, and your thoughts run perpetually on food ... you dream of imaginary meals, you remember past meals, and you wonder how in the world you can manage to secure a little extra something for the next meal.

Not long after our arrival, Len went to join some friends of his another part of the camp. He had been a staunch companion during our misadventures, which I should not have cared to experience without him. His messmates helped him with money, which he very generously shared with me; with ten dollars in my pocket, I felt justified in joining two friends in the hut who were messing together. They were E.H. Williams, the Puisne Judge in Hong Kong, and Colin Morrison, a young government cadet. Victor Fasciato, agent for a Sheffield steel firm, joined us a little later, and we stuck together throughout our stay in Sham Shui Po. We shared out any extra food which we managed to scrounge, and I tried to earn my keep by appointing myself odd-job man to the mess.

Life for me took on a much brighter aspect as the food problem became
less acute. The rations, too, improved gradually; beans and vegetables
were added to the menu, and after a month or so we were even given
a little meat now and then. Our staple diet was still boiled rice, and
remained so throughout our imprisonment. The ration gave you a feeling
of reasonable repletion after a meal, but owing to its high percentage of
water it was very quickly digested, and within an hour or so you were as
hungry as ever.

We did not only go short of food; our captors stinted us of all the
necessities of life. But prisoners become very ingenious, and an astonishing
variety of make-shifts was produced. Empty tins were fitted neatly with
handles and made into mugs; tables and stools were constructed from
odd bits of wood, and nails picked up around the camp; windows were
shuttered with matting and corrugated iron; when boots wore out they
were replaced with home-made wooden clogs, or patched with rubber cut
from the tyres of derelict buses. Three of the latter had been abandoned
on the main parade-ground, and provided a gold-mine of useful bits and
pieces. In spite of strict orders that they were not to be touched, they
gradually melted away, and little was left except the frame and heavy
engine castings.

We stuffed rice-sacks with coir to make mattresses, and when the hot
weather came we made sheets from flour-bags. Some ingenious person
introduced an immersion heater for boiling water, and soon every mess
was constructing its own out of bits of wire and empty tins; highly
dangerous affairs, which were constantly fusing or giving us shocks. They
consumed a most satisfactory amount of Jap current, and were of course,
strictly prohibited. That first winter, however, no current was available,
and for light we relied on miserable little home-made lamps burning oil
which we scrounged from the invaluable motor-buses. I was always a
good sleeper, and could spent most of the dark hours in blissful oblivion;
sometimes, though, I would lie awake, passing the time by re-living past

holidays. On one of these occasions I heard a plaintive voice from our sergeant-major, who talked in his sleep, saying "Boy! BOY! Whisky Soda!" Poor fellow, he couldn't make the pace, and died after a few months' imprisonment.

At first there were some 5,000 troops in camp. These consisted of the survivors of the 1st Batt. Middlesex Regt., the 2nd Batt. Royal Scots, the H.K.V.D.C., and detachments of all the various corps and units normally stationed in Hong Kong. The R.N. and the R.A.F. were also represented. There were large numbers of Indian Troops, but these were soon transferred to another camp. The Royal Rifles of Canada and the Winnipeg Grenadiers, who had arrived in Hong Kong only a fortnight before the invasion, were at first confined at North Point on Hong Kong Island, but were later moved to Sham Shui Po. The officers were imprisoned with the men … and unusual arrangement in P.O.W. camps … and were responsible to the Japs for our discipline. Subsequently most of them were transferred to a separate camp at Argyle Street, Kowloon.

The POW camp at Argyle Street, Kowloon (from the August 1944 issue of the Far East Special Monthly Edition of *The Prisoner of War* published by the POW Department of the Red Cross and St. John War Organization) *[10]*

The Volunteers were a regular League of Nations. Most of us were men like myself, who had come out from the British Isles to make a living in the Colony … civil servants, business men, engineers and professional men of all sorts. There was also a strong and very keen Portugese contingent, many of whom had lived all their lives in Hong Kong. They were a great asset to the camp, for they kept fit on the whole, and were invariably cheerful. Many of them had artistic talents, and our concerts and shows would have been poor affairs without them. A number of Eurasians and Chinese had also joined up to defend their home town; of these, the Chinese were liberated in the summer of 1942; we didn't envy them … they were likely to find life in the town a good deal harder than in prison.

In addition to these groups, there were individuals from all over the world … Russians, Scandinavians, Frenchmen, a Belgian, a Czech … even an Austrian and a Hungarian. The Russians were interesting fellows, resigned to a life of trouble, for most of them had fled from the Revolution and worked their way down the China coast from Siberia.

Elsewhere in the camp were some American seamen, a Red Indian and an Esquimaux half-breed. Yes, all the world had arisen to cry "Halt!" to the aggressors.

Incidentally, the oldest man in camp was over seventy, the youngest under seventeen. A grandfather and grandson, and several fathers and sons were imprisoned together.

Various officers commanded the Volunteers at one time or another. Of these I would mention Capt. Valentine for the kindly interest he took in each individual member of the Corps. But all these officers would willingly admit, I think, that our real leader was R.S.M. Jones, late of the East Surreys, who was with us throughout our imprisonment. At first we chafed under the military discipline which he had to enforce, but he understood men, and underneath his barrack-square manner lay a strong sense of humour. This was invaluable to him in dealing with an awkward crowd like the Volunteers … ex-civilians accustomed to having their own way. By degrees we all came to respect him for his absolute impartiality and honesty … qualities which are none too common in a P.O.W. camp. Discipline was maintained in the Volunteers, and it was the right sort of discipline; we obeyed the R.S.M. not by compulsion, but because we wanted to; we realised that his orders were for the common good.

And no trailing off to hospital for him when he felt sick and weak; his spare, upright figure always turned up on muster parades. No timid subservience to the Japs … or to anyone else for that matter – when the welfare of the Volunteers was in question. A man on whom we could rely.

Prisoners hate change, and much of our discomfort was due to a passion of the Japs for playing general post with all the troops in camp. At an hour or so's notice we would have to pack all our belongings and shift to another hut. This happened with distressing frequency; I think I slept in thirteen different huts and rooms during my stay in Sham Shui Po. For this reason it never seemed worth while doing any unnecessary work on our temporary abodes; no natty wall decorations, curtains, pipe-racks or bric-a-brac for us. We became resigned to frequent moves, and most of us refrained from collecting a lot of junk which would have to be carted away about camp every month or so. But it was discouraging to start afresh in a completely bare hut, and sometimes the previous occupants were not at all helpful; some of the regulars were once caught pushing a bath out of a third floor window in Jubilee Buildings, apparently just to spite the people who were taking over the flat from them.

After a few weeks in the Theatre hut, I was moved to an even colder and noisier hut in the lines. A few days later, however, I joined my messmates in a small room facing the main road, which we had to ourselves. This hut measured about 16 ft. by 8 ft. and the majority of the floor space was occupied by three army beds and my mattress – I had not yet acquired a bed. We made window shutters and a door from sacking, corrugated iron and bits of wood. Washing lines were strung from wall to wall, and festooned with a squalid looking collection of towels, dishcloths and spare clothes. On a shelf were our mess-tins, mugs and a few odd bottles of curry powder or soya sauce … anything strongly flavoured helped down the rice. A rickety table and two or three small stools completed our furniture. In a corner was a fireplace constructed of a half dozen bricks, on which we used to brew tea of cocoa when such luxuries were available. The smoke went up into the roof, and often descended into the next room, where it caused much coughing and blasphemy.

Orders were periodically issued forbidding small fires, but they were ignored, and some eptitious fires used to burn merrily in the huts throughout our stay in Sham Shui Po. A certain British officer used to prowl round the roof of Jubilee Buildings trying to spot offenders by watching for smoke from the chimneys. This anti-social behavior did not increase his popularity. In our hut Williams, lately the terror of thieves and malefactors, brought before him in the Supreme Court, was now the most adept scrounger for firewood. He would obligingly help a fatigue party to demolish a damaged hut, collect a huge armful of timber in an offhand manner, and slink back with it to our room.

The days passed extraordinarily quickly, for there always seemed something to do, some kind of occupation was the best antidote to boredom, depression and hunger. Household chores had to be done … washing dishes, sweeping out the huts, washing and mending clothes, odd bits of carpentry and tinkering. Then there were lengthy parades and fatigues, of which I shall have more to say later. A large portion of our time seemed to be spent in queues; we queued for meals, long lines of hungry men standing with clinking mess-tins outside the cookhouse in the cold wind; we queued at the wash taps, we queued at the M.I. room, we even queued at the latrines.

CHAPTER 4

REACTIONS

"The whole atmosphere of prison, even the most easy and best regulated prison, is odious. Companions in this kind of misfortune quarrel about trifles and get the least possible pleasure from each other's society"
— *Winston Churchill*

"My God, I've learned something about human nature … and about myself" said a friend of mine when I met him again after a long separation in different prison camps. Hardship reveals a man as he really is, and it was interesting to watch the reactions of my fellows – and of myself – to prison life.

Most of the Volunteers and Canadians, and many of the Regulars, had been pitched into warfare on December 8th for the first time in their lives. There followed eighteen days of uninterrupted retreat, with all the disorganization and despondency, which, I should imagine, inevitably result from a hopeless rearguard action. The retreat ended in a last stand at Stanley, the surrender of Hong Kong, and the rounding up of all the surviving defenders. When these men arrived in camp they were in a mood of disillusionment about the defence of Hong Kong, the army, and the war in general. Anyone of discernment had seen for months past that the Colony could not be held for long against a full-dress attack, for it had been left with totally inadequate naval and air support. The policy of the authorities seemed to have fallen between two stools; why, we asked ourselves, had they not provided Hong Kong with adequate defences, or declared it an open city? I suppose that war materials and men were too urgently needed elsewhere to provide an adequate garrison here, while to leave the place entirely undefended was not in keeping with British prestige.

It was a bitter business, though, for the defenders of Hong Kong; they felt that they had been bamboozled by the authorities, and made up their minds that henceforth they would treat official utterances with extreme caution. Here is an example of the way in which the troops were fooled: shortly before the surrender an official statement was issued, and published in one of the last issues of the South China Morning Post, to the effect that a large Chinese force was advancing over the border, and that if only the troops could hold out for a few more days they would be relieved. This report was without foundation; I was shut up within sight of the border at that time, and it was quite obvious that there was not the least hope of a Chinese attack.

Everybody was naturally swapping war reminiscences during the first few weeks in camp, and some thrilling tales were told. I will not, however, try to write a second-hand account of the Hong Kong campaign.

Though we were disillusioned when we arrived in Sham Shui Po, we were by no means despondent. Wildly optimistic rumours quite unfounded, flew around the camp … "Wavell has reached Indo-China", "Churchill has promised that Hong Kong shall be relieved within three months", "The Volunteers are going to be released to run the essential services in town", and so on. One hopeful fellow even sent out a message to his amah to get his flat ready, as he would be coming back to it in a week or so. The stock greeting was "It won't be long now".

For most of us in the Volunteers it was a big change in our way of living; a few weeks ago we had been dwelling in comfortable homes, with well-trained servants to attend to our wants; now, all of a sudden, we had to fend for ourselves, destitute and comfortless. It was astonishing, when we bothered to think about it, how little we were concerned about the loss of our homes and all they contained in the general smash-up. We could not do anything about it, and the question of possible compensation in the distant future assumed far less importance than the immediate question of the next meal. We were still alive and kicking ... that was the main thing.

At first I felt just like Mr. Bultitude in "Vice Versa", the somewhat pompous and self-satisfied middle-aged man, who magically changed places with his school-boy nephew; he found himself bereft of all his treasured privileges, comforts and responsibilities, a very unimportant member of the school, harassed by pettifogging rules, and chivvied all day long from one uncongenial task to another. Yes, it was very like being a fag at school again ... very humbling. The experience was certainly very good for us, but it went on far too long.

And it was not only the Japs who humbled us; some of our own officers were apt to forget that we had recently been responsible citizens in Hong Kong, and treated us as kids of twelve. A reasonable amount of discipline was obviously necessary, and we were quite ready to submit to it, but all sorts of exasperating and futile little restrictions were imposed; in these early days we were never allowed to forget that we were in the army now. How bored we were by the well-meant little pep-talk given by our worthy company commander every morning on parade. Then there were endless fatigues ... an army system specially designed to prevent anyone taking any pride in his work. Nobody objected to doing the routine jobs essential for the camp, but it did seem rather superfluous to cart a lot of broken bricks from one dump to another.

Again, the daily "detail" was a perennial source of amusement or irritation, according to your temperament. These were orders and instructions emanating from the Japs or from our own staff, and often utterly footling ... "Newspapers will be cut into four-inch squares when required for toilet paper" …fancy, you wonder what things are coming to! It wasn't as if there were any drains to be blocked.

Generally we obeyed the more reasonable orders, and simply ignored the stupid ones, but you often heard remarks to the effect that "If this is the way the ---- army is run, no wonder it loses every battle except the last one!". It was just as well, however, to heed the bloodcurdling threats issued from time to time by the authorities against anyone breaking Japanese military law.

Sham Shui Po Camp by Lt. A.V. Skvorza *[11]*

Many of us were new to barrack-room life; we were overcrowded, and had to adapt ourselves to this uncomfortable existence, trying not to be irritated by the funny little ways of our neighbours, and to suppress irritating little ways in ourselves. In our diminutive hut there was no room to spare, and the resulting compression occasionally produced a certain amount of heat. Morrison disliked draughts, while I disliked fug; our door consisted of a double thickness of sacking, and I made myself unpopular with him by appropriating one thickness to make into a mattress. He in turn used to annoy me by hungrily scraping his spoon around inside his mess-tin long after he had extracted from it the last grain of rice.

Fasciato was a warm-hearted and cheerful individual; his only failing was a certain crustiness in the early morning. "Good morning, Fash!", I used to say when we woke up. "Don't be so damned hearty", he would reply ... "It's a b----- awful morning".

Sometimes there were brief rows, which cleared the air, and must have provided much amusement for our next-door neighbours. Our friendship was unshaken: indeed it grew closer as the months went by. We came to have a great affection for Williams; he was older than the rest of us, more steady-going and sensible, and became the father of our mess.

Human beings are adaptable creatures, and we soon settled down to make the best of the new conditions. After the fall of Singapore we gradually came to realise that we were in for a long stay; well, we should just have to be patient. Sensible folk adopted the point of view that "this is my life for the time being; I had better make the best of it. Come day, go day, roll on the time of my release."

When would it come? If only we could have looked forward to a definite date! On muster parades I used to look round at my fellow prisoners, rank upon rank of them, and think what an appalling waste of manhood this forced inactivity entailed. Here were fine men whose brains and talents were going to rust; youngsters who should have been entering life with zest; ordinary solid fellows, good husbands and fathers, who might have been doing a useful job of work; old chaps who had surely earned peace and comfort. It was not much consolation to remember that this wastage was world-wide.

I remembered being taken to see a performance in Manchester of a tense one-act drama about P.O.W.'s translated from the works of one of those gloomy continental writers, and produced by an extremely earnest company of amateurs. It was a dismal November evening as we walked from the tram-stop through dim streets down by the Irwell, that sad little river that looks as though it were filled with ink. We entered a tall, forbidding building, and groped our way up to a kind of attic fitted up as a theatre. The audience, who evidently considered themselves to be intellectuals, were taking their places on the hard benches.

The curtain went up on a dimly-lit scent representing a drab prison hut. The setting however gave me a not inaccurate prevision of a Sham Shui Po hut on a black-out evening. Throughout the play, three bearded and unkempt prisoners sat on boxes and discussed their miserable lot. They were hopeless chaps; nothing went right with them; one man's sweetheart had committed suicide, another had lost his job, and the wife of the third had run away with someone else; the future was grim and glum.

I often thought of this play during our imprisonment, and thanked my stars that it didn't take us that way. Most of us kept our self respect and our sense of humour; loud burst of laughter were frequently heard in the camp; people would break into a song, or whistle when they did their washing-up. Life was still worth living, and the future was still full of hope.

No, provided we could keep reasonably fit, we seldom suffered from acute despondency. It was only that we lived "luke warm". For a while – so long a while – we remained in a state of suspended animation, like hibernating animals. We never experienced those rich moments of ecstasy, which in the old life used sometimes to come unsought; as when we heard great music, or watched the pageant of dawn from some high peak, or fell in love. The real zest of life was gone for the time being.

How did prison life affect character? Did it weaken our moral fibre as it weakened our bodies? In the first place I think it stripped most of us of a lot of humbug. We were reduced to the common level; we dressed in the same odds and ends of uniform; distinctions of class or race or wealth disappeared. The pretentions of civilized life were gone; the poseur cut no ice, we saw our fellow-men as they really were.

I might be thought that this was a real opportunity for a communal effort. Here was a closed community in which everyone (not counting the officers) started from scratch in a state of almost complete destitution; why should we not share and share alike in the matter of food and amenities, and unite in trying to work out in that way, and the result illustrates the futility of communistic attempts to level all men to the same standard. Grant them equality of opportunity, by all means, but you will never get equality of wealth. And so it was in Sham Shui Po; differences soon began to appear; the determined and unscrupulous soon found comfortable berths and extra food for themselves, the lazy and faint-hearted sank into a hungry, hugger-mugger existence, while the best among us plodded quietly along, trying to help their fellows in an unobtrusive sort of way.

In a very real sense, the fittest survived, for we were back in a primitive state where the instinct of hunger was all-important. The feckless soon became dirty and unkempt, sold their kit for cigarettes, and when they were reduced to rags took to stealing to satisfy their craving for smokes. When fags were scarce, these people would sell excellent greatcoats, battle-jackets boots and so on for two or three packets of cigarettes.

Shaggy, untidy-looking men would even dog the footsteps of Jap officers, in the hopes of picking up a fag-end or two. I remember one soldier whom we called "the missing link" on account of his uncouth appearance. He used to spend his time slouching around the lines looking for cigarette ends; his total equipment consisted apparently of a shirt and slacks, a blanket and a grubby towel. He used to draw his rations in a tin tray and a mug; he would use his hand to scoop his rice from the tray into his mouth, they wipe the tray with his towel, and return it to its place under his bed.

It was will-power that counted in the struggle to keep going. There were some poor chaps who, although suffering from no disease, failed to adapt themselves to a rice diet, gave up the fight, fell ill and died of malnutrition.

But the great majority of the prisoners came through the test with courage and determination. They kept their self-respect, and managed to turn themselves out reasonably smartly, in spite of the shortage of soap, razor-blades and tidy clothes. They took some pride in keeping their bed space and meager possessions in good order. They practiced thrift and patience. They kept fit if they possibly could, but if they fell ill and went to hospital (as nearly everyone did sooner or later), they were determined to get well and return to the lines. Courage, cheerfulness and generosity shone like lamps in a gloomy world.

During the war a party of R.A.M.C. men were rounded up by the Japanese, who, to save the trouble of taking them into captivity, beheaded them all save one. The latter, a Corporal Leath, was left for dead on the ground, with a severe wound on the back of his neck. He was subsequently taken to hospital, where he made a complete recovery, and served as an orderly during the latter part of his imprisonment. The following verse, which he wrote in somebody's autograph book, shows the light-hearted way in which people put up with things ...

> "I nearly lost my head by Gad;
>   I sometimes wish I really had;
> But luckily I lost no teeth.
>   Yours sincerely,'
>   N.J. Leath."

Chapter 5

Escapes and Departures

"During great injustices, increase thy patience, and the injustice shall not touch thy soul" – Leonardo da Vinci

King's Regulations do not enjoin patience in a prison camp; it is a prisoner's duty to escape, if possible. During the first few months there were several successful escapes, for the Japs had not yet instituted any efficient means of checking the number of prisoners in camp. Each company commander was supposed to call the roll every morning, and report all present to the Japs, but if two or three of his men had disappeared overnight he naturally fudged the return.

One lucky man found it absurdly easy to escape. He was a Chinese volunteer, and had relatives in the town. One day they came to the fence, and handed over a basket containing civilian clothes and an overcoat. While the sentry's back was turned, he slipped these on, climbed through the wire, and disappeared unobtrusively in the crowd outside.

Soon after my arrival, I came across Dr. Ride, of the University, standing by the fence and looking gloomily out to sea. We greeted each other, and he remarked that what with dirt and flies the camp would be a death-bed when the hot weather came. Next day he was gone; he had managed to charter a junk, and escaped in it with a small party, which eventually reached Chungking. Fortunately he remembered our encounter, and it was through him that my family first learned of my safety.

Sham Shui Po Camp in 1942 *[12]*

As a result of these and other escapes, the Japs gradually tightened up restrictions. Trading and the handing over of parcels over the fence was stopped, but an enterprising sampan-man used to bring a cargo of tinned goods at 4 a.m. to the little slipway at the western corner of the camp. We used to stand there in the darkness, waiting our turn to step down to the water's edge and haggle, while one of us stood guard on the sea wall above, dimly silhouetted against the sky. The prices were staggering, but the sampan-man did a roaring trade for a week or so; eventually he became nervous, and refused to risk his neck any longer.

Muster parades were instituted to check the escapes. These were a sore trial at first; we would fall in, to begin with on our company parade ground, and be numbered, then march to the battalion parade ground, where we were numbered again; finally we would march the length of the main road to join the muster of all the units in camp. There we might spend an hour, several hours, or even most of the day, standing in boring discomfort on the glaring parade ground, while the roll was called or a search was made. But by degrees things became better organised, until the regular morning and evening musters occupied only a quarter of an hour apiece.

Sham Shui Po Camp roll call by Lt. A.V. Skvorza, 1944 *[13]*

Often there were inspections; the camp area would have to be tidied up, huts cleaned out, beds folded. We would curse because all washing lines had to be taken down, and we could not dry our clothes or air our blankets. Then would follow the usual lengthy muster parade, and at last, after several false alarms, the Big Noise himself would appear, attended by a retinue of lesser noises. He would glare sternly at the ranks of prisoners, make a rapid tour of the camp, and depart.

On one occasion the newly-appointed Governor of Hong Kong inspected us. He was accompanied by a bodyguard … a lorry load of thugs bristling with arms. In the old days of the wicked British Administration, the Governor used to go about the Colony attended only by his A.D.C.; in fact the misguided Chinese seem to have regarded him with respect and affection. Strange that they did not now realize how much better off they were under the Co-Prosperity Sphere!

Later on the camp was inspected twice yearly by Mr. Zindel, a Swiss resident of Hong Kong, who represented the International Red Cross. He used to be escorted by the Camp Commandant and other Jap officers, and, as far as I know, no prisoner was ever allowed to converse with him. But no doubt he used his eyes, and it must have been to him that we were indebted for the gradual improvement in our lot; we should have been in a poor case had it not been for the efforts of the various Red Cross organisations.

There was a certain amount of "look-see pidgin" about these inspections. I remember that a quantity of attractive looking foodstuffs was once brought into camp by the Japs, and arranged tastefully in the main kitchen and ration store before the arrival of the inspecting officer. Nobody was allowed to touch them, and that evening, after his departure, they were all taken out again.

An escape which took place in March was treated very seriously; we were roused in the middle of the night by the bugle sounding "Fall in at the double", and scrambled out of our warm and comparatively comfortable beds to spend an interminable time on the parade ground. Some friends of those who had escaped were taken out of camp and severely handled. Collective punishments were enforced; the recently instituted canteen was closed, and no parcels were allowed to be sent in by friends in the town. This did not affect me, as I received only one private parcel during the whole of my imprisonment. The idea of punishing those who had not transgressed was quite an effective one, for you were much less likely to escape if you knew that the friends you left behind you would consequently get even less to eat than before.

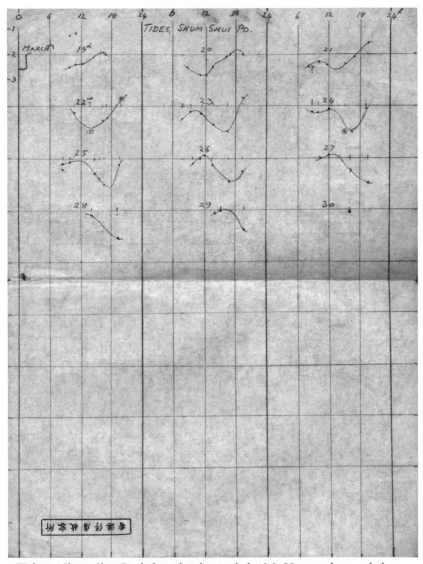

Tides at Sham Shui Po, believed to be made by Mr Heywood, recorded on a piece of paper from the POW camp labelled in Chinese meaning "Hong Kong Prisoners of War Internment Camp". The tidal record was for a continuous period from the 19th to 30th of the month of March – could this be related to the escape which took place in March 1942, mentioned above?

In April nearly all the officers were transferred to Argyle Street, another prison camp in Kowloon. We thus came directly under Japanese discipline, and expected trouble. But our fears were groundless; on the whole the Japs interfered little with our daily life, and we suffered less from petty militarism now that our own officers were out of the way.

The Japs appointed a British liaison officer to run the camp under their orders. They chose wisely from their point of view, for their underling was a "yes-man", who thought only of pleasing the Japs, and nothing at all of the prisoners' welfare. Each night he used to make the rounds of the camp, checking the numbers in the huts, until everyone's relief the Japs ceased to supply him with torch batteries, and his prowlings had to cease. He would take part in searches, and we used to see his tall nervous figure emerging from a hut, followed by a satellite with an armful of loot … a pair of pliers, some wire, a hammer or two or some immersion heaters … treasured but illicit possessions which had not been sufficiently well-hidden.

It was hardly surprising that he became the most unpopular man in camp, and was referred to in a sermon one Sunday morning as "the Judas in our midst". He blocked any suggestions for improvement where a go-ahead and determined man might have done a great deal to better our position. Admittedly he filled a most unenviable position, but he filled it very badly.

At about this time I managed to obtain a permanent job in the camp garden, where I spent my mornings trying to grow sweet potatoes. I enjoyed the work and the comparative solitude; it was far preferable to lining up at the morning "slave market" after muster, and being detailed for some dull fatigue. I shall be able to sympathise with the casual labourer in future – also, incidentally, with the washerwoman; I detest washing clothes.

Another advantage of being a gardener was that I was occasionally rewarded with some sweet potatoes as a perquisite; we used to boil these over a small fire, and share them out in the mess.

By degrees we were allowed various amenities; books were brought in, concerts and games arranged, a canteen opened, and so on. I shall have more to say about these in a later chapter, but here I should like to put in a word of praise about our original camp band, which did a great deal to cheer us up when things were looking black. They played us on to parade, they accompanied the hymns in church, they gave open-air concerts on summer evening, and they played to the patients in hospital. One of their favourite tunes was "Happy Days are here again" – hardly appropriate, perhaps, but anyway it was a good rousing air.

Band at Sham Shui Po Camp (from the April 1944 issue of the Far East Special Monthly Edition of *The Prisoner of War* published by the POW Department of the Red Cross and St. John War Organization) *[14]*

Food improved; we now had three meals a day, and flour was added to the rations. A bakehouse was constructed out of odds and ends by the engineering experts; our bakers turned out sufficient bread to give every man half a loaf per day. The rations were now about 1 lb. of rice, 10 oz. of bread and some vegetables daily; 5 oz. of meat twice a week, dates occasionally. We seldom went hungry on this diet, but it was ill-balanced and unsuited to European stomachs; we were soon to experience the results of prolonged underfeeding, and very unpleasant they were.

Solitary confinement must be a terrible punishment; when we were feeling low we could at any rate cheer ourselves by chatting with our friends. Small talk took up much of our time, and trivial incidents occupied our attention; we would rush to the door to see the rations arriving at the kitchen, or an aeroplane passing overhead. A whole hut would take sides, quite amicably, in tremendous arguments which did not matter two pence to anybody.

And the gossip! Never tell me that women are worse gossips than men. Each of us would have done well to have had the Three Monkeys as his mascot. You find them in curio shops in the East – one holds his hand over his eyes, another over his ears, and the third over his mouth, … "see no evil, hear no evil, speak no evil!". It was always a lot easier to sit back and criticise the quarter-master or the cooks than to set to and do some useful job yourself; Sham Shui Po was full of armchair critics. This carping at others is often, I think, a sign of a feeling of frustration; by running the other fellow down you endeavour to gain self-importance. Perhaps we were all feeling frustrated and humbled – we had cause to be.

The Japs were still worried about escapes; the barbed wire fence was doubled and increased in height, and buildings standing near it were demolished. Look-out towers were built, and the perimeter was lit at night. Later, the inner fence was electrified; a prisoner accidentally met his death through electrocution while cleaning a nullah near the fence.

In May an order was issued that we must all sign an undertaking not to attempt to escape. We assembled on the parade ground, and awaited the arrival of Col. Takunada, the commandant of all the Hong Kong prison camps. He was a very stout individual, with an absurd little squeaky voice, and a great sense of his own importance. In spite of his unprepossessing appearance he was comparatively harmless, and was known to the troops as "The Fat Pig".

On his arrival, he mounted a table, called for a general salute, and proceeded to address us through an interpreter. "You British prisoners must OBEY! If you refuse to sign this paper, it will be regarded as MUTINY, and you will be punished according to Japanese military law".

There followed much subdued discussion in the ranks. What did the funny little man mean by "mutiny"? Mutiny, we supposed. Was this a parole, to be taken as binding? Ought we not to leave ourselves free to attempt to escape should an opportunity arise? What were the officers going to do? But there seemed no alternative. The officers decided to submit, and, following their example, we all filed past the Jap officials and signed the undertaking, with the mental reservation that it was obtained under duress and was not binding.

The Japanese punishment for minor offences was slapping. This could be quite an ordeal. The culprit, standing stiffly to attention, was dealt a succession of stinging blows on the face, which as often as not knocked him down. He would then be kicked or dragged to his feet again, and the slapping repeated half-a-dozen times. It was galling, and you did not incur such a beating-up if you could avoid it. But at any rate you had the consolation of knowing that this was the normal punishment in the Japanese army, and that the sentries were slapped just as often as the prisoners.

My own experience of slapping was a mild one. I was sleeping out one hot night on the ground in front of our hut; all around were other sleeping figures, but unluckily I happened to be just in the path of some sentries coming off duty. I was unceremoniously kicked awake, hauled to my feet, and given one good stinging slap before being hustled with my bedding into the hut.

Far more serious punishments were incurred by anyone implicated in attempts to escape. Some civilian internees, who had been recaptured after escaping from Stanley, were formally tried, and sentenced to two years' imprisonment with hard labour. We heard that they were under close confinement, subsisting on starvation diet, and undergoing terrible hardships. It seemed unlikely that they would survive their sentence, but they did.

On the whole, though, I think that such privations as we suffered were due to indifference rather than to malice. During the first few months of their occupation of the Colony, the Japs obviously had to content with great difficulties of organisation and supply. Also we were apt to forget that their normal standard of living was much lower than ours; we were not much worse off than their own garrison troops, and certainly far better off than thousand of starving Chinese in the town.

I do not love the Japanese – I never did, even in peace time, for they were such officious little blighters – but they are human, like the rest of us, a mixture of good and evil. Only they have a thinner veneer of civilisation than we. Undoubtedly they committed some atrocities during the taking of Hong Kong, but how many successful armies can claim a clean record in this respect? On the credit side, most of us could tell of little kindnesses shown to us by our captors. I shall have something to say later of a camp commandant who was a really kindly man, respected and liked by all of us.

All the same, we were badly underfed, we were neglected, and the camp hospital was a disgrace.

In July the Volunteers moved to Jubilee Buildings. I well remember sitting on a pile of our squalid-looking belongings, waiting for the previous occupants to clear out before we would take possession. Rain was threatening, and we looked and felt just like evicted slum-dwellers.

This move unfortunately interrupted the activities of a party who were planning to escape by the traditional method of tunneling. They occupied part of a ground-floor flat in Jubilee Buildings, facing the sea, and were engaged in driving a tunnel from the back premises of the flat towards the sea wall, which was built of massive granite rocks. But they were discovered and taken out of camp. Three subsequently returned after being beaten up; we were given to understand that the remainder had "died of malaria".

The Sham Shui Po military camp and Jubilee Buildings in the 1930s *[15]*

We were still overcrowded in Jubilee Buildings, sleeping eight or ten in a small room, but we had the luxury of cold baths and flush sanitation. Williams discovered a razor for me, and I was able to shave off my horrible beard, which had never looked either well-trimmed and debonair, or bushy and venerable; my friends were as glad as I to see it go. Moreover, I had at last acquired a bed – a rickety affair constructed of wood and wire netting – and during the hot weather I slept very comfortably on an open verandah. There was only one snag about my bed, which it had in common with every other bed in camp. A casual visitor to Sham Shui Po (if there had ever been one) on a fine summer day, would have been surprised to see here and there a prisoner lugging a heavy iron bedstead out on to the concrete pavement. He would then pull it to pieces, lift each piece above his head, and dash it madly to the ground with a shattering clang. Next he would execute a kind of step-dance, stamping around the bit of bed, before repeating the banging process. He would examine every part minutely before fitting the bed together again and returning it to his hut.

Yes, you have guessed aright ... he was carrying out his weekly de-bugging. Every summer these loathsome pests invaded our quarter; we could keep them in check by ceaseless vigilance, but could not entirely get rid of them until the cold weather put a temporary stop to their activities.

Fortunately very few of us entertained those other guests which are apt to impose themselves on the soldier … lice. There was plenty of running water, and no one had any excuse for failing to keep his clothes and person reasonably clean.

During the heat of summer we were more comfortable in one respect than we had been in peace time; we could go about all day with hardly any clothes on. For muster parades we had to wear a cap, shorts and singlet, but for the rest of the day most people wore nothing but a pair of shorts, or a "fandoshi" – a kind of cotton loin-cloth supplied by the Japs. To save wearing out our boots and socks, we took to Chinese clogs, or simply went barefoot. We weren't ornamental – an underfed prisoner in a fandoshi is not an impressive sight – but we were comfortable, and acquired a tan which would have been the envy of the most ardent sun-bather.

The first draft of 600 prisoners to be transferred from Sham Shui Po sailed for Japan in August. No Volunteers were included and the draft was made up largely of the scallywags of the camp. Certainly discipline improved after their departure. We had suffered a lot from petty thefts; towels and clothes disappeared from washing lines, and one night a shadowy figure stole into our hut, pinched a pair of boots from under Morrison's bed, and was away before anybody was awake enough to catch him. Worst of all, a bag of treasured tinned goods belonging to our mess was stolen from our room in Jubilee. We decided that, if any extra food came our way in future, we would store it at once in our stomachs.

In September another draft of nearly 2,000 men sailed for Japan in the "Lisbon Maru", which was torpedoed and sunk by an American submarine when a few days out from Hong Kong. The news cast a gloom over the camp; it seemed such a wretched futile waste that these lads should be drowned through the action of our Allies, after suffering the war and months of imprisonment. Many good friends of mine were on board; we were left in doubt as to their fate until after the war, when the Japs at last sent in casualty lists.

Left: A list of the *Lisbon Maru* victims from the Sham Shui Po camp, written by Heywood.
Right: A proposal for a memorial tablet for the *Lisbon Maru* POW Rover Scouts victims who were part of St Andrew's congregation, found in Heywood's archives.

The camp was soon filled up again by the arrival of the Canadian prisoners from North Point. They were mainly youngsters unused to soldiering; they had reached Hong Kong only a fortnight before the invasion, and were not acclimatised to the tropics. Consequently there was more sickness and distress among them than amongst the remainder of the prisoners. They stuck it out, tough, most of them, and towards the end the Canadian working party included some of the fittest men in camp.

One incident has not been mentioned in this chapter, as I did not hear any details of it until after my release. During 1943 plans were made for an escape on a grand scale. Most unfortunately these were discovered by the Japanese, and four officers and a number of other ranks were taken out of camp. They were ill-treated for several months, starved, tortured and finally tried. The officers were condemned and executed; to the last they refused to implicate any of their fellows, and each was posthumously awarded the George Cross after the war.

HONG KONG PRISONERS OF WAR CREW. ROLL AND RECORD.
Chaplain — Rev. C. Strong.   R.S.L — G. Heywood.

Name	Unit.	Previous Crew or Date Invested.	Camp-craft.	Pioneer-ing.	Handi-craft.	Crew Practices.	16-Mile Hike.	Swim 100 yds.	Hygiene	First Aid.	Citizen-ship.	Recruit (Optional)	Remarks.
ARCHER, A.	R.N.	Deep Sea Scouts											Left Camp. 25/9/42. *
BAILEY, G	R.A.M.C	Rover Sea Scouts							P				
HAWKSWORTH, W.	R.N.	Deep Sea Scouts											Left Camp. 25/9/42. * A.R.S.L.
MACKENNY, W.	R.N.	"											Left Camp. 25/9/42. *
NEWINGTON,	R.E.	"											Left Camp. 25/9/42. *
PENDLEBURY, W.	R.N.												Red Stripe.
CAINE, R.	R.E.	St Andrew's	P	P	P	P	P	P	P	P	P	P	Red Stripe. Left Camp. 23/9/42. +
CARROLL, G.	R.Signals	"	P		Aug. '42	P	P	P	P				Left Camp. 25/9/42.
DARBY,	H.K.V.D.C.	"											Left Camp. 23/9/44
LOCKHART, T.	H.K.V.D.C.	"	P			P		P		P			Left Camp. 13/12/43 A.R.S.L.
MATTHEWS, C.	D.D.C.	"											Left Camp. 4/42.
MAYCOCK, R.	H.K.V.D.C.	"											
MILLINGTON, L.	H.K.V.D.C.	"											Left Camp. 19/1/42.
MILLINGTON, V.	H.K.V.D.C.	"											
RAMAGE, H.	R.E.	"											Left Camp. 25/9/42. * Rambler's Badge
TAYLOR, A.	R.Signals	"											Left Camp. 25/9/42. Rambler's Badge, Red Stripe
TOMLINSON, J.	R.Signals	"	P	P	P	P	P	P	P	P	P	P	Left Camp. 25/9/42. *?
CHORLEY, G.	R.Scouts	Rover Sea Scouts											Died, March 1942.
GIBSON, R.	R.Scouts	"	Aug. '42					P				P	Left Camp. 25/9/42. *
HARRISON, H.	R.E.	"											Left Camp. 25/9/42.
KIM, G.	R.N.V.R.	"	P	P	P								Left Camp. 25/9/42. Rambler's Badge, Red Stripe.
LONGSON, R.	R.E.	"	P	P	P	P	P	P	P	P	P		Left Camp. 12/12/43
MAYLE, W.	R.Scouts	"											Left Camp. 25/9/42 Rambler's Badge, Red Stripe
NOLDE, N.	R.E.	"	P	P	P	P	P	P	P	P	P		
WILKINSON, G.	R.Scouts	"											Left Camp. 25/9/42. Rambler's Red Stripe.
WHITMORE, J.	R.A.O.C.	"	P	P	June '42	P	P	P	P	P	July '43	P	Left Camp. 12/12/43
ROBERTSON, J.	M/x	1st Edgeware											Left Camp. 13/12/43
IRESON, V.	R.E.	23/2/42											Left Camp. 25/9/42.
PALMER, R.	R.E.	23/2/42.											Left Camp. 25/9/42
CRABB, F.	H.K.V.D.C.	7/3/43	Aug. '42										
CURLEY, J.	R.A.M.C.	"							P	Aug. '43	P		
ORCHARD, W.	H.K.V.D.C.	"	Aug. '42										
CRARY, D.	H.K.V.D.C.	21/5/43											Left Camp. 12/12/43
HEWITT, R.	R.A.O.C.	"			Sept '43	Sept '42							Left Camp. 12/12/43
INGLEBY, W.	R.A.P.C.	"											Left Camp. 13/12/42
LYLE, I.	R.A.P.C.	"			Sept '43								Left Camp. 13/12/43
WHITE, A.	H.K.V.D.C.	"											Left Camp. 23/6/44
DUNLOP, R.	R.R.C.	8th Stamford (Canada).											
AUMONT, G.	R.R.C.	5/8/43											Left Camp. 15/9/42
MARSOLAIS, H.	R.R.C.	"											Left Camp. 15/9/42
TAILFORD, S.	R.A.F.	"											Left Camp. 10/9/42
DODD, J.	H.K.V.D.C.	20/8/43											Left Camp. a/a/43
HEADFORD, J.	R.N.	"											Left Camp. 12/12/42
KEDDIE, J.	R.Scouts	"			Sept '43	Oct '42							
SMITH, J.	R.A.O.C.	"									Jan '44	Jan '44	

While Heywood did not mention much about scouting activities in this manuscript, his meticulous recording of the status of his fellow Rover Scouts clearly indicates that such activities were carried out rather systematically inside the camp. Names marked with asterisks or crosses were on the *Lisbon Maru*.

CHAPTER 6

MALNUTRITION

"It causes pain, but it doesn't hurt ... One confuses hurt and pain – pain is nothing. Hurt you must consider as injury, vital injury, the loss of hope or courage" – Henriques

It was during this first summer that the effects of Malnutrition began to show. Although by now we were generally getting enough rice to produce a feeling of repletion after meals, it was poor fare. The meat allowance dwindled away and finally vanished, and for a long time were we vegetarians, until the Japs began to send in an occasional ration of fish. Summer is the off-season for vegetables in Hong Kong, and to help the rice down we were given some entirely tasteless greens, used by the Chinese in normal times as pig-food. The leaves and hollow stalks of these when boiled provided a concoction known as "Green horror" or "whistle-pipe stew".

The diet was mainly starchy, and deficient in fats, proteins and vitamins. Unfortunately, the rice we ate was polished; this process, so our doctors told us, deprives it of the vitamins B1 and B2, which are present in the unpolished grain. Consequently, although we were not desperately hungry, we nearly all began to develop some form of beri-beri or pellagra. These diseases are due to a deficiency of the B vitamins, and are prevalent

A ROVER CAMP OF LONG AGO

On the day of the Japanese attack on Pearl Harbour, 7th December, 1941, the 1st St. Andrews Rover Crew , Hong Kong, were encamped high up on the slopes of Kowloon Peak, a few miles from the town. It was a beautiful site, with a wide view over the hills and islands and sea-inlets along the S China coast. The weather was perfect, sunny and cool, as it usually is in December in Hong Kong, and we were enjoying a thoroughly pleasant week-end.

We were a cosmopolitan bunch; British, Eurasian, Chinese, a White Russian and a Norwegian, all getting on very happily together. Perhaps half our number were Army men from the garrison in Hong Kong.

We had just finished breakfast on that Sunday morning when a messenger from Army H.Q. came panting up the path with orders that all Army personnel were to return to barracks immediately. The Service men hurriedly struck their tents, packed their rucsacks, said good-bye regretfully and disappeared down the path. One thing they left behind was a lovely great piece of beefsteak, intended for Sunday dinner, which they stuffed into a billy and buried in a corner of the camp-site, in the forlorn hope that they might come back next week-end and enjoy it.

The rest of us struck camp that evening and went home. The following day the Japs invaded the Colony, and three weeks later, after the fall of Hong Kong, we were herded into prison camp or internment camp. Our diet for the next 3 years and 8 months consisted mainly of rice; meat was a rare luxury, and our thoughts often turned longingly to that lovely round of beef lying buried on Kowloon Peak, with nobody to eat it.

G.S.P.H.

An interesting story of a piece of beefsteak lying buried by Heywood's Rover Crew up on Kowloon Peak on the day before the Japanese invasion – often remembered at the Sham Shui Po camp where meat was a rare luxury

in countries where polished rice is the staple food. They first appeared about six months after we had come on to this diet.

We had none of us realised how extremely unpleasant malnutrition is, for these diseases manifest themselves in all sorts of painful ways. When you are half-starved, you don't merely grow thin and hungry. Some people developed defective eye-sight, others got sore mouths which made eating a torture. Then there were nasty skin troubles … boils, rashes and septic blisters that refused to heal; we know now why Lazarus was afflicted with sores. The excessive amount of water contained in boiled rice resulted in grotesquely swollen ankles; if you pressed your finger into them, the dint remained. But the most trying complaint was "Aching feet", which would be difficult to beat as a form of slow torture. It started as a dull ache, as if you had just been a long walk in ill-fitting shoes; then shooting pains like toothache would assail your toes, and finally the nerves in legs, hands and arms would be affected. It was pitiful to see men in the prime of life hobbling about like old dodderers. At night they would get no rest; they would sit up rubbing their feet, or walk to and fro for hours, or sit on the edge of a wash basin with their feet in cold water to numb the pain.

It was fatally easy for a man to go downhill. A slight stomach trouble, perhaps, or a bout of malaria or dysentery, might start his decline. His appetite failed; he pushed half his rice away untasted, and lost weight until he became a tragic figure, little more than skin and bone. One poor fellow weighed only 50 lbs at his death. Many men, however, refused to give in; uncomplainingly they endured long months of pain and weakness, until conditions improved and they began to recover.

Malnutrition was a polite word for starvation; yet even in these days there were some who could keep fit on the diet, provided they were lucky enough to avoid sickness, and had trained their long-suffering stomachs to assimilate as much rice as they could push into them. Some men always remained well-covered, capable of a day's manual labour.

Dysentery was on the increase, and we were warned to keep our eating-utensils scrupulously clean. We waged a successful war on flies; at one time they were very numerous, and the Camp Commandant awarded a packet of cigarettes for every hundred dead flies. 16,000 corpses were handed in on the first day, and the offer was hurriedly withdrawn. It was rumoured, probably quite untruly, that some enterprising regulars were starting a fly-breeding establishment with which they hoped to keep themselves in fags.

Worst of all was an outbreak of diphtheria; many good men were carried off before the Japs could be persuaded to supply anti-diphtheria serum, and almost every day we saw sad little funeral processions going out of the camp to the cemetery. To check the spread of infection, we were all provided with small cotton face-masks, such as you often see worn in Japan. We were supposed to keep these on day and night, but I'm afraid we didn't. Gargling was instituted, the serum arrived, and the epidemic was at last controlled. It had been a bad time.

Hospital conditions were deplorable; the various huts used as wards were always overcrowded, and it was impossible to keep them clean; a peculiar musty smell hung about them. Not until we had been imprisoned for a year did the Japs fit the hospital huts with windows. Till then the frames were shuttered with sacking and corrugated iron, and the wards were dismal indeed. In these discouraging surroundings, our doctors from the R.A.M.C. and the Volunteers struggled against disease, handicapped by a lack of drugs and medical supplies of all kinds. Major Ashton Rose, of the I.M.S., was appointed senior medical officer by the Japs. He was an autocrat, but he knew how to deal with Asiatics. He was not to be put off by their exasperating way of saying "Very sorry; tomorrow, maybe", but went on worrying them until, sometimes, he got what he wanted. He reorganised the wards, scrounged drugs and extra food for the sick, and started a large and flourishing vegetable garden for the hospital. He would chivvy lazy convalescents out of bed and into the sunshine, with excellent results.

Major Gray, another of our doctors, who in peace-time was a pathologist at a big London hospital, constructed a yeast-plant which provided a daily ration of yeast for every man in camp. The yeast was brewed from fermented flour and sugar, and supplied much-needed vitamins which undoubtedly helped to check deficiency diseases. "Elevenses" at the yeast bar became a popular feature, which unfortunately came to an end after a few months owing to a shortage of flour.

During the first year, you were no better off in hospital than in the lines, unless you were seriously ill. You avoided muster parades, it is true, but there was nothing extra to be had in the way of food or medical supplies. Serious cases were later transferred to Bowen Road Military

Hospital, where the wounded prisoners were housed and conditions there were better than in camp.

Bowen Road Military Hospital c.1910-20s *[16]*

I escaped lightly this first year. One day early in the summer a friend remarked "My word, Heywood, you are getting dark!" I replied that I had been working out in the sun all day, and was acquiring a very fine tan. "Maybe", he said; "but it looks damned awful to me".

Some-what piqued, I borrowed a mirror, and found that I was indeed a revolting yellowish-grey colour. It was an attack of jaundice; heaven knows how I caught it ... certainly not from over-eating. I soon recovered, though for a month or so my friends continued to tell me that I looked terrible. However:

"My face, I don't mind it,
For I am behind it,
It's the people in front get the jar!"

This was the only trouble I had in 1942, apart from pitching head first into a deep concrete nullah. My head healed up in a few days but a graze on my skin took seven weeks. Septic sores are the devil on a low diet.

Our fortunes were at a low ebb in November, owing to bad food, overcrowding, and heavy working-parties; nearly everyone was suffering from malnutrition in some form or another. But just when the outlook was blackest, our captors began to distribute a large shipment of Red Cross supplies. Blessing on the Red Cross organisation! It undoubtedly saved our lives. There were quantities of bully beef, M.&V., tea, sugar and cocoa. There was atta, a kind of wholemeal flour which made excellent porridge, and ghee, which resembles lard. Bales of clothing and boxes of medical supplies. Best of all, we each received an individual parcel … a big one, stuffed with good things. Our spirits soared, and there was an immediate improvement in health.

Some money was distributed, and we were able to buy smokes and a few groceries at the canteen. The first fried egg for a year was indeed a treat! So our second Christmas in captivity was quite a festive affair, notable for three delicious meals which included not a grain of rice.

CHAPTER 7

WORK

"Let them be hewers of wood and drawers of water"
– Old Testament

"Show a leg; it's 4:30!" said the night-picket, shaking me by the shoulders; "Don't miss your breakfast".

Having satisfied himself that I was awake, he went back to his draughty vigil on the stairs outside the flat. I scrambled out of bed and dressed hurriedly, muttering curses against the Japs for making me get up at this unearthly hour. Better not put my boots on yet … might wake the others. I slipped on a pair of clogs, grabbed my mess-tin and mug, and stumbled out into the starlit night. Joining the crowd round the dimly-lit kitchen hatch, I drew my breakfast of rice and vegetable stew, together with my picnic lunch of a couple of rice cakes and a vegetable pasty.

Back in the flat, I ate a hasty meal, which could be hardly said to fortify me for a day's work. There was just time to pull on my boots and pack my haversack, before joining the shadowy crowd of prisoners assembling on the parade ground. Our long-suffering R.S.M. sorted us into parties of a hundred, and we proceeded to await the convenience of the Japs for the best part of an hour. I lay down on the ground, with my water bottle for a pillow, and slept while the stars paled in the dawn.

Working parties in the early days had been comparatively mild affairs
… in fact men often used to volunteer for a day's digging in order to
enjoy a jaunt outside the camp. But now, in October 1942, the Japs were
busy enlarging the airport at Kai Tak, and demanded big parties every
day. Consequently every fit man, not engaged on essential camp duties,
had to be out from before dawn till after dark, with one day off in four or
five. On a rice diet, this was a heavy strain.

At last the sentries arrived; we were counted again, and herded on
board a ferry steamer which had come alongside the jetty. It was a tight
fit, for we were six or seven hundred strong. Luckily I found myself room
to curl up on the deck and go to sleep again, amongst the legs of the
benches and the boots of my companions. For I was in no mood to
watch the harbour slipping by – that harbour which a year ago had been
so full of life. In those days perhaps a hundred ships might be in port,
many of them busy loading or unloading cargo; ferry steamers bustled
to and fro, launches tooted impatiently on their various errands, and the
brown sails of innumerable junks and sampans added a decorative touch
to the cheerful scene. Now the Blight had settled on the harbour, and it
was dead. Most of the small craft were gone; half-a-dozen dingy tramp
steamers lay at anchor, as many more lay on the mud at the bottom of
the harbour, with only the tops of their masts and funnels showing above
the water. Much better to sleep, and perhaps to dream of England, and
dear ones, and good meals.

A voyage of an hour brought us to the pier at Kowloon City, where
we were somewhat cheered by a sentry dropping his rifle into the sea. We
disembarked, fell in to be counted again, and marched in a straggling
column to the scene of our labours. A few friends and relatives of our
local lads had turned out to watch us pass, and waved to us from the
pavement.

After yet another count – a prisoner spends much of his life being
counted – we eventually started work about half past nine. We were

Kai Tak Airport in 1942 *[17]*

employed on an extensive scheme for enlarging Kai Tak airport. At first we had been set to shifting granite blocks – all that remained of a demolished village. The work had not been well organised, and we managed to go slow with some success; with luck you could even steal a break now and then, to recline at ease in the shade of a rock. But now we were engaged in demolishing a hill, and each gang had a definite quota of earth to shift during the day.

I provided myself with a spade, and set to work filling baskets with earth from the excavation and tipping them into trucks. When these were full, the excitement began. Each truck was manned by two or three of our more adventurous youngsters, who when it was loaded, removed the chocks, pushed off down the rails, and sprang aboard. Away they went with shouts of glee for an exhilarating run of a quarter of a mile down to the marshy fields where the earth was unloaded. The gradient was fairly steep, the lines ill-laid, and the braking arrangements crude, so it was little wonder that there were some mighty crashes. A heavily-laden

Sacred Hill in the early 1900s (above) [18] – the boulder bearing the three carved characters "Sung Wong Toi" (宋皇臺) was situated on top of the hill (below) [19]. The hill was levelled and the boulder was broken up by the Japanese in blasting operations to extend Kai Tak airport.

truck would get out of hand, and its crew would leap for safety, yelling a warning to anyone down the line; the truck would go careering on, to collide with a most satisfying crump against the train unloading at the bottom, sending it somersaulting down the embankment. Fortunately there were no fatalities, though one day a driver broke his leg.

While the trucks were being unloaded, we had a short breather; soon they were back again, and we resumed picking and shovelling. It was a glorious autumn day, and we worked in the blazing sun, stripped to the waists. I could keep on shovelling at a steady pace without becoming unduly exhausted, but I was not really fit for heavy work and felt slack and listless; the morning seemed endless.

At last the bugle sounded for lunch; we broke off, and hurried across to draw tea, which was boiling in a large oil drum over a fire. I went back to the shelter where I had left my haversack, and squatted down to eat. The lunch-hour would have seemed quite a pleasant picnic if the food had been more alluring.

Most people had managed to save up a cigarette to smoke after lunch, and we sat around and yarned.

"Supposing you had a drug which would put you gently to sleep for six months" said one, "would you take it?"

"I don't think I would" replied one of our optimists, "We might be out by then, and I should hate to miss getting home."

"I'm not so sure", said another, "Sleep is certainly the best way of passing the time here, but this is the only life we've got at present, and on the whole I think I would rather be conscious than unconscious".

If we had known that we should not get out for nearly another three years, I feel sure we should have all voted for the drug.

"By Jove, you know"' continued the first speaker. "We'll have to watch our step when we go home; my language is getting dreadful."

"Oh you'll soon mend your ways in polite society. But I'm wondering what my wife will say when I start collecting cigarette ends from the ash-trays, and smoking them in my pipe!"

"Won't it be wonderful to sit in an armchair again!"

"Yes, and to find chairs wherever you go, instead of carting a beastly little home-made stool around."

"And no queues for meals; and as many second helpings as you like."

"Bacon and eggs for breakfast."

And so the talk drifted to the ever-fascinating subject of food, until the bugle summoned us unwillingly back to work.

Keep going steadily now, and don't waste any energy; we have got to fill thirteen train-loads today, and we have only sent down six so far. It was the hottest time of day, and the bare ground reflected a dazzling glare into our faces. My gang was working on a miniature cliff, about twenty feet high, which the pickers were beginning to undercut considerably. This was the quickest way to obtain our quota of work, for if we had worked down from above we should first have had to clear away a mass of undergrowth and tree stumps. But these earth cliffs are apt to collapse. I did not like the look of it, and protested, but the pickers preferred to go on taking chances.

In the middle of the afternoon there was a short break, when gangs of once-respectable citizens of Hong Kong, clad in shorts and little else, sweating and weary, might be seen lining up for the reward of their labours … two cigarettes and half-a-dozen boiled sweets. When we returned to camp, we should in addition receive 10 sen each, at that time worth considerably less than a penny.

After drawing our pittance and another mug of tea, we sat down to rest in such patches of shade as we could find. Suddenly, without the slightest warning, the whole cliff-face above us came down with a muffled rumble, burying the working site under many tons of soil. It was only by the mercy of Providence that it had not collapsed earlier in the afternoon, and that no one happened to be sitting under it when it did come.

Anyway, we could now fill the trucks from the fallen earth without the trouble of picking it. The end of the day's work seemed not too immeasurably remote.

Soon after 4 p.m., the British lieutenant in charge of the working party had a word on the quiet with the Chinese overseer, while there were no Japs about. He spoke Cantonese, and had a way with Asiatics which he often used to our advantage. He managed to persuade the overseer to fake in an extra train-load on his tally-sheet, which meant that we could knock off after completing one more load. We roused our flagging energies, sent down our last trucks with a cheer, and stacked our picks and shovels well before the bugle sounded at 5.

We collected our kit, fell in to be counted again, and marched off down the lane, our sentries trailing along with fixed bayonets on either side of the column. The heat of the day was over, and soon, blessed moment, we reached the shade of the houses, where I could take off my dark glasses and rest my eyes at last from the glare. We clattered on board the ferry, and settled ourselves with muscles comfortably relaxed for the voyage back to camp. This was the best time of the day; I fished a book from my haversack and read for a while, then watched the sun setting in glory behind the hills of Lantau Island.

Back in camp, we fell in to be counted for the sixth and last time that day. What was that faint, alluring odour wafted towards us from the kitchen? Could it be fish for supper? It was, and before long, bathed and changed, I was sitting down to a good big helping of rice and a tasty bit of fish fried in batter. After supper I smoked one of my hard-earned cigarettes, and turned in early, for I was detailed for another day's work at Kai Tak on the morrow.

No, the Kai Tak working parties were too much of a good thing. You felt that they were almost worth it, though, when your turn came for a day off, and you could lie in bed until 8:30 a.m., and spend the day in lordly idleness. A lot of our pleasures in Sham Shui Po were of that sort … like that of the man who, when asked why he was banging his head against a brick wall, replied that it was so nice when he left off.

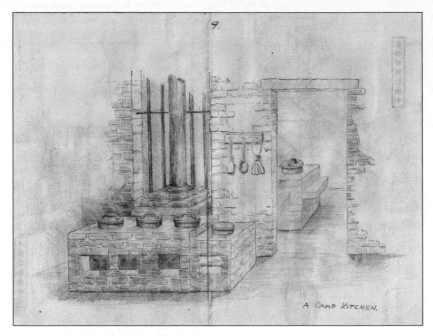

Sketch by Heywood – A Camp Kitchen

Fortunately the Kai Tak job came to an end at Christmas and though the Japs subsequently employed working parties in all sorts of ways, the hours were much more reasonable.

Apart from these, there were numerous jobs to be done in camp. Permanent staffs were employed in the Kitchen, Bakery, Hospital, R.A.O.C. Stores, Boot-mending Shop, Garden, Farm, Library and so on. In addition there were many prisoners employed as batmen, office assistants, and sweepers and cleaners about camp. Lucky was the man who could work his way, by "friend-pidgin" or palm-oil, on to the kitchen staff; he was safe from malnutrition. Much ill feeling was aroused by the practice of some unscrupulous members of the kitchen staffs of stealing food-stuffs, such as cooking oil, and selling them in the camp. A bad business, but let me be honest, and confess that sometimes I have had a bit of extra chow, wangled by a friend with a friend in the kitchen or bakery, or pocketed as perquisites in the garden. It is an imperfect work, and not many could lay their hands on their hearts, and swear that they had never eaten a mouthful more than their rightful share of the food from the common stock. As time went on and things became better organised, these rackets were suppressed, and the food coming into camp was fairly distributed; we could never be sure, though, how much of our rations had been diverted by our captors before they came into camp.

Latterly the staffs of the two main cookhouses, under Potuloff and "Busty" Bowers, could pride themselves on their honesty and fairness, and did a hard and thankless job of work extremely well.

It was a good thing to get a permanent job, if possible. You could take some pride in your work; time passed more quickly when you had regular hours, and you could plan your days in some sort of routine; best of all, you seldom had to go on working parties, and were spared the soul-destroying "casual-labourer" jobs in camp, such as carting bricks about, emptying latrine buckets, cutting grass with a blunt table-knife, and so on. Unfortunately, I was prevented by sickness from continuing work in the camp garden, but when I finally left hospital early in 1944 I obtained a job as batman to a disabled officer, which kept me going not too strenuously until my release.

CHAPTER 8

ROLL ON THE YEARS

"And party leaders you might meet, in twos and threes in every street"
– W. S. Gilbert

We had now been prisoners for a year; the Blight had spread over the whole of the Far East, and the day of release seemed even more remote than it had when we first came in. A few irrepressible optimists, however, were still saying "It won't be long now!" Indeed they continued to do so throughout our imprisonment.

And while we were condemned to years of futility, the Allies were fighting to check aggression, fighting to keep our families safe, fighting to hasten the day of our liberation. I think that we were sometimes too wrapped up in our own troubles and forgot that in this war others were undergoing severer trials than we.

Shortly after Christmas, 1942, I went down with malaria, and spent the following year in and out of hospital with recurrent attacks of fever.

On January 19th the third draft sailed for Japan. 1,200 men left us, including many Volunteers: among them, alas, was Williams, whom we missed sadly from our mess. We said goodbye to him on the main road in the darkness of early morning; he was glad to go, for most people thought that if the draft reached Japan safely they would find better conditions there. Against this there was always the hope that Hong Kong would be relieved before the end of the war, resulting in the earlier release of the Sham Shui Po prisoners. In one respect, Williams was lucky, for this was the "Show Draft"; its members were provided with a complete kit, including greatcoats and even a pair of white gloves, and they travelled in the "Asama Maru", before the war one of Japan's crack liners. After they had gone, we shifted our abode once more to a different part of the camp, and as usual had a heavy job clearing up the mess left by our predecessors.

A new Camp Commandant arrived, who, unlike the previous one, really took some interest in our welfare, and a long period of peace ensued, with fewer annoyances such as moves, extra parades and petty restrictions. Concerts became a regular feature, more books were brought in, people began to make their own gardens, and the Red Cross supplies were lasting out. As a result of the better conditions, the health of the camp improved.

Malaria, however, pulled me down; I could not get the wretched bug out of my system, and grew weak and scraggy. Then I began to have skin trouble – an uncomfortable, humiliating business. My behind was sore, so I couldn't sit down, blisters broke out on my feet, so I couldn't walk about; then sores appeared on my hips, so even bed was uneasy, and I began to wonder whether I should have to spend my time standing on my head. I would be awake half the night itching, and with my hands bandaged. I could not even wash properly. It was very trying.

The doctors and R.A.M.C. orderlies did their best, but external treatment was of little use … what I wanted was a course of bacon and eggs. They tried scrubbing me down to clear off the surface infection. It was a most undignified proceeding; a burly ex-prison-warder set to with a hard brush on my naked form, and scrubbed till I was raw. He meant well, but worked far too energetically for my liking.

I was beginning to fear that I should go down with general blood-poisoning, when Morrison came to my rescue with a dozen assorted

Strehticide tablets. How he managed to collect them I do not know, for there were none in the hospital dispensary. They just turned the scales in my favour. But enough of this "organ recital"...

Of camp life in general during 1943 there is little to record. Apart from the upheavals caused by occasional drafts to Japan, our captors left us very much to our own devices; musters became shorter, inspections fewer, and working parties less arduous. Mercifully there were no attempted escapes. I know it is the duty of a P.O.W. to escape and rejoin the fighting forces; but perhaps his duty lies the other way when his chances of getting through occupied China are extremely slim; he is liable to be shot on recapture, <u>and</u> some of those he leaves behind may die of malnutrition owing to the cutting of rations as a collective punishment.

At all events, most of us had quite given up the idea of escaping; for any hope of success we should have had to possess bodily strength, a stock of provisions and cash, and a knowledge of the Chinese language, and it was impossible to get together a party having all these qualifications.

The great excitement of the year was the bombing of Lai Chi Kok oil depot in September. We had become accustomed to the visits of "Albert", the American reconnaissance plane which used to fly unconcernedly to and fro over Hong Kong in broad daylight. He was above A.A. ranges, and no fighter ever challenged him. The deep drone of his perfectly tuned engine was as music in our ears. Then there had been a few sporadic raids, which, though apparently not very effective, were most comforting to our morale.

But this was a different affair altogether. Our friends from inland came over high one fine day, and dropped a beautifully aimed salvo plumb on to the oil tanks of the depot, which stood about a mile away across the bay, in full view of camp. A colossal column of smoke and debris rose impressively hundreds of feet into the air, and a glorious bonfire was started, which burned merrily for four days. A gale, providentially springing up after the raid, spread the conflagration, and we learned later that nearly all the tanks were destroyed.

Subsequently a brief notice appeared in the "Hong Kong Daily News", the news sheet published in English by the Japanese, stating that, owing to unforeseen circumstances, the bus services would be suspended indefinitely.

This miserable little paper now came fairly regularly into camp, and we could discern the main events of the war in Europe and the Far East through a haze of the most unblushing propaganda. We were to understand that the entire American Navy had been sunk several times over; yet, curiously enough, the fighting seemed to draw nearer and nearer to Japan. Hong Kong was said to be flourishing as it never had in the bad old days of the cruel British domination; yet the price of rice continued to rise, and more and more people starved.

From information which we gleaned from time to time, these were some of the benefits of the "Co-Prosperity Sphere": Hundreds of thousands of Chinese citizens of Hong Kong had been "repatriated" … in other words, kicked out. The military yen, which replaced the Hong Kong dollar, was steadily depreciating in value, and was to become practically worthless before the end of the war. The harbour was idle, and road transport seemed to consist of rickshaws, tricycles, and a few coolie-drawn wagons. It was proudly announced in the paper that the latter were equipped with hand-brakes! Later, the electricity supply was entirely cut off, owing to the coal shortage … so helpful to industry! Robbery and violence were rife, and in some cases convicted thieves were sentenced to death. The newspaper did not tell us, of course, of the thousands who must have died of starvation, but working parties when they went out of camp used to see corpses lying for days unburied in the streets. So much for the "New Order" in East Asia.

A bout of malaria in November was my last, for by then the proper drugs had been obtained, and a course of these cleared me of the germs.

To my great delight I was transferred to the "Malnutrition Ward" to convalesce – for my ribs were sticking out like a railing. There we were given a little extra food, which Major Ashton Rose had somehow managed to procure; half a pint of milk on most days, a small extra ration of fish and cooking oil, and occasionally tomatoes from the camp garden or a little pork from the camp farm. It was not much, but just enough to make all the difference, and I began to pick up.

Sketch: My Bed-space, March-October 1944

I spent my third Christmas in captivity in this ward, and was finally discharged from hospital in March, 1944. It was pleasant to return to the lines, and cheering to think that I was classed as a fit man once more, in spite of disadvantages such as night picket duty and muster parades. Some people were quite content to remain in hospital month after month, not exactly malingering, but making no effort to get fit. The one great aim in everyone's mind was to walk out of the gate as fit as possible when the day of liberation came. Maybe the best way of attaining this was to lie on one's back doing nothing for as much of the time as possible, but most of us preferred a more active existence; there was no time for boredom and depression in a day well filled with activities.

It was glorious to feel fit again; I put on weight, my skin cleared up, and I could sleep blissfully the whole night long. I was lucky enough to obtain a permanent job as batman to Lieut. Thomson of the Royal Scots, who was disabled by the loss of one eye and injury to the other.

My friends pulled my leg about this job; they remarked that when my offspring asked "What did Daddy do in the war? The reply would be "Oh, Daddy was captured on the very first day, and became an unofficial, unpaid, underfed private attached to the Hong Kong Volunteers. He was an undergardener for a while, did various coolie jobs, then rose to be a batman, and became quite good at house-work." "But I thought Grandpapa was a Colonel in the last war but one." "Yes, things were different then."

Anyway, I was in good company, for many important citizens of Hong Kong were serving as privates in the Volunteers.

This arrangement worked excellently as far as I was concerned, for all sorts of little extras came my way; never tell me again that Scotsmen are ungenerous. Soon after I took on the job I committed a fearful faux pas, for which a less indulgent employer would have sacked me. One morning I went to draw his breakfast as usual from the kitchen. His porridge was collected in a large enamel mug, fitted with a lid to keep out the flies; this I handed in at the kitchen hatch, and turned away to chat with someone. The breakfast was served; I picked it up (as I thought), took it to the officers' hut, and set it on the table. Returning thither after my own breakfast, I thought there seemed to be a slightly ominous silence in the hut. The boss, without looking up, said "You can have what's in my mug; I don't want it."

"I say, that's awfully kind of you," I replied, adding somewhat insincerely "I hope you're not off your food."

With my mouth watering at the thought of a second breakfast, I took the lid off the mug ... and found it half full of tepid tea. Everybody in the hut was laughing, so, endeavouring to hide my disappointment, I said "It's lucky you weren't hungry this morning; there seems to have been some mistake over your porridge."

"I <u>was</u> hungry, and I'm hungrier still now! It was an extra special porridge, with bran and ground beans in it, and I would like to know what the hell has happened to my ration."

Mumbling apologies, I snatched up the mug and dashed off to the kitchen again. This was terrible; to deprive a man of his ration is the worst thing you can possibly do in a prison camp.

"Oh, yes; we were expecting you" they said at the kitchen. "You picked up the wrong mug this morning."

I know, confound it. Well, what's happened to Mr. Thomson's ration?" It appeared that there wasn't a drop.

Eventually I took my trouble to Potuloff, the head cook. He was a large and genial Russian, who in peace time had been manager of the Lido at Repulse Bay; he did wonders with his scanty supplies, and no rackets went on in his kitchen. After listening sympathetically to my tale, he unearthed a helping of porridge, which I believe was his own breakfast ration. I took it back in triumph to the officers' hut; Mr. Thomson had his breakfast after all, and we lived happily ever afterwards.

Our mess was now reduced to Morrison and myself, for the genial Fasciato had sailed for Japan on a recent draft. We were in a hut which held twenty men at a squash; we continued to be overcrowded however many drafts went away, for those that remained were packed into a smaller and smaller area of the camp. We sometimes wondered whether the last remaining prisoners in Sham Shui Po would finally inhabit a small wired-in hut in the middle of the camp, surrounded by a wilderness of empty buildings and deserted vegetable gardens.

We went through some thin times in the summer of 1944. The rice ration had been reduced, the Red Cross supplies had long since been exhausted, and we all felt hungry. Then, quite unexpectedly, lorries came into camp one evening in August, bringing a big consignment from the Canadian Red Cross. For once there was no lack of volunteers for the fatigue party to unload them, and until long after dark a cheerful gang was busy stowing away quantities of exciting-looking bales and boxes. When, after maddening delays, the distribution had finally been arranged, each man receiving three individual parcels, with an additional two to be divided amongst every three men. This was superb! We unpacked our parcels with as much excitement as children at a school-feast; those lovely big tins of dairy butter and powdered milk could be made to last for weeks; and what did it matter that the cheese was a bit weevily … we scraped off the weevils and ate it.

The consignment also included a generous supply of clothing, medical stores, books and sports gear. Thank you, Canadian Red Cross!

At the same time the Japs, unpredictable creatures, sent in some delicious frozen meat … game, liver and tongue. We owed this treat to a discontinuance of the electrical supply in the town, and the consequent failure of cold-storage plants.

Everybody cheered up wonderfully, and, to add to our satisfaction, the news from Europe was most encouraging; the tide had turned at last, and was rolling back in full flood across the plains of France.

Here is an account of a day in camp at this period:-

October 16th, 1944. Reveille at 6:30; I did not hear a sound until roused half-an-hour later by a cheerful voice bellowing "Chow up, number five!" Just outside the hut. Translated into English, this means that it was time for number five party, to which I belonged, to draw their breakfast. Scrambled out of bed, seized my utensils, and made for the kitchen clad in my night attire … a ragged old vest and pants.

We filed through the kitchen to draw our pint of ground-rice porridge, ladled from a big cauldron, and as much plain tea as we wanted. The latter was brewed in an old bath. Breakfast in the hut, each man sitting on his bed. Today there was a little bran in the porridge, and I added some Canadian powdered milk. Meals are usually eaten in silence; unsociable, perhaps, but eating is too important a business to be interrupted.

After breakfast I had time to dust and sweep my bed-space, tidy up, and shave, before we fell in outside the hut under our Party leader for muster at 8 a.m. We marched to the main parade ground, all out of step, and formed up in fives.

"Volunteers … 'shun! Right … dress" from R.S.M. Jones. We don't mind making some smartness on parade for him, but we would not do it for anyone else.

"Come on, wake up there, so-and-so! You're not still in bed! Eyes front. Number … Stand at ease."

After a few moments of lively chatter, the bugle sounded and the Japs came on parade. Honda, the acting camp commandant, marched down the line, accompanied by the Liaison Officer; the latter an unhappy-looking man whose duties seemed to press heavily upon him. They were followed by a Jap interpreter and a sentry with fixed bayonet. We were called to attention and numbered as they passed; the numbers tallied satisfactorily with Honda's lists, and soon the bugle sounded again, and we re-formed in open order for twenty minutes' P.T.

Sergeant Major Pacey, our P.T. instructor, mounted the dais, and the band stuck up. It sounded rather thin and reedy in the open air, consisting as it did of some strings, an accordion, a saxophone, a cornet and a drum. We marched, countermarched, and carried out some easy exercises without much enthusiasm, the early sun casting long gesticulating shadows on the bare red earth of the parade ground.

It will be noted that a somewhat Nazi tinge had crept into the colour of our existence; we were no longer organised in companies, but in "parties", each under a party leader; we indulged in mass-callisthenics; the sentries goose-stepped when they passed an officer. The Japs are born copy-cats, and no double picked up these ideas from their German instructors and advisers.

After P.T., the "employed" men were dismissed first; I bustled away with the crowd and queued up outside the R.A.M.C. hut to draw my daily vitamin capsule – for which we were indebted to the Canadian Red Cross.

Then to the officer's hut, where I carried out my batman's chores. It was Monday – washing day – so I bundled my master's washing together with mine, and pounded them in cold soapy water in the wash-house. My best efforts failed as usual to impart a snowy whiteness to the washing, but at least it didn't smell by the time I had finished with it. By 10:30 the washing was hung up in the sun, and my morning jobs were over, so I returned to my hut to enjoy the first cigarette of the day.

For most of the rest of the morning I was far away in spirit from Sham Shui Po, happily buried in a technical book; thank heaven one can still go on learning in this place! Considerable concentration was required, however, for our room had twenty occupants, and seldom were they all quiet at one time.

Lunch at 12. Salt-fish "chow-fan", consisting of boiled rice heated up with a little oil and scraps of dried fish; coffee, for a treat, from my last Red Cross parcel. After lunch I sat back for a while on my bed, smoked half a cigarette and read a novel. Then across to the officers' hut to wash up. I generally used to read to my boss for an hour or so in the afternoon, but today he was playing bridge, so I returned to my hut to write up this journal.

Later … This was intended to be an account of an ordinary day, but it turned out not to be so ordinary after all. I had just gone out to do a little gardening when the air-raid warning sounded. We all hustled into our huts, and in ten minutes or less we could hear the unmistakable sound of approaching American bombers.

Everyone crowded to the windows, talking excitedly.

"They're coming, boys; they're coming!"

"Can you see them?"

"Not yet … Yes, I can now … coming straight overhead. One, two, three, … it's a big formation of bombers. I make it twenty-eight altogether, not counting those fighters in attendance. By Jove! this is the biggest raid we have had yet!"

Air raid by American B-24 Bombers on 16 October 1944 (Hong Kong Island in left foreground, Stonecutters Island to left of middle, Kowloon in middle with New Territories behind the mountains) *[20]*

I just caught sight of them, gleaming in the blue, high overhead, and decided that a lot of rubbish would soon be descending from the skies. We had only a thin wooden roof over our heads, so, following the example of another steady-going married man, I retired underneath my bed. The latter was an ancient army one, and for the first time in my prison life I blessed that iron-clad piece of furniture; with mattresses and a pile of blankets on top it would stop quite a lot of falling debris.

The youngsters in the hut were jumping to and fro between the windows and the open door. " Hullo; are you comfortable under there?" said one of the cheekier ones.

"Quite, thank you; tell me what's going on."

"Come and see for yourself. You won't get hit unless the bomb has your name on it!"

"Well, I'm taking no chances. It would be just too bad to be bumped off in an Allied raid."

The windows rattled with the rumpus of A.A. fire and distant bomb explosions. Suddenly there was a shout from the door: "Look at this! My God, look at this! You can even see the stars on their wings!" Six light bombers had surged over the Kowloon Hills, and were roaring down across camp at a height of only a few hundred feet. As they passed overhead, they let fly with their machine-guns at the shipping in the harbour. Everything opened up at them, even the sentries popping away with their rifles; there was a terrifying racket, but in a minute the Americans were away out of sight beyond Green Island, unscathed.

Sure enough, a lot of bits of metal fell in camp, and a few people were slightly wounded. Honda came round the huts directly the raid was over, before the all-clear, to ask if there were any casualties. He is a really nice man; a kindly thought like this makes a world of difference.

A pipe-full of cigarette ends helped to while away the rest of the afternoon; the all-clear very obligingly sounded just in time for us to go and draw our supper at 5 p.m. Everybody, of course, was delighted at the raid, but we breathed more freely now that it was all over.

Supper ... rice, bean stew, plain tea, with a smoke to follow. Then across to the officers' hut to clear up, make the Boss's bed and take in the washing. There was still time to do a little work in my garden; on a perfect evening like this, it is pleasant to potter around among my plants.

7 p.m. ... Evening Muster; this only took ten minutes or so, and I returned to my garden to plant some sweet-potato cuttings given me by Len Starbuck. We have no lights nowadays, so I had my cold shower and got ready for bed before it grew quite dark. Tucked up snugly inside my mosquito net, I ate a little left-over rice (it was a long time between supper and breakfast), smoked the last of my daily ration of three cigarettes, and entered into a desultory conversation with the fellow in the next bed.

9:30 p.m. ... "Lights out" on the bugle, and I fell asleep almost at once. But the day's activities were not quite over, for I was detailed for night-picket from 11:20 to 12:40. Each hut was to post a picket throughout the night, presumably with the idea of setting a thief to catch a thief, and so preventing escapes. Another crazy scheme of the Japs; after all, it is their job, not ours, to stop people escaping. Night pickets are a bore, but one's turn only comes round about once a week.

The fellow on first watch woke me; I dragged myself from the depths of slumber, pulled on a pair of shorts over my underclothes, and tottered round to the main door of the hut, where I took over the official armlet from my predecessor. The night was still and warm, and I spent my shift pleasantly enough watching the constellations which looked, remote and aloof, on the sleeping camp.

Bed again. The day had been fully occupied, and so had slipped by reasonably quickly. Those Yankee pilots were pretty brave, I thought. Lucky blighters; hours ago now they would have been back at their base, eating a jolly good supper. What couldn't I do with steak and onions ...

those luscious brown sausages we used to get at Wenlock … a marmalade pudding cooked by my wife … Stilton cheese …… I was asleep.

Yes, I know, food plays a disgustingly large part in this chronicle. But this is a true story, and I want to convey to you that the subject of food occupied our thoughts very often indeed. Ascetics claim that their meditations become more rarified and spiritual as their stomachs become empty; I don't believe it.

4 Far East MAY, 1945

CONDITIONS IN HONG KONG

PRISONER OF WAR CAMPS AND MILITARY HOSPITALS

Information from a reliable source about the Hong Kong Camps has now become available. This is a summary covering broadly the period from January, 1942, to July, 1944.

FOOD

AT the end of December, 1941, the food position was described as shocking and all the prisoners soon began to show the ill effects of this. Constant representations by the camp doctors did, however, achieve some modifications and small improvements.

During the early part of 1943 the prisoners' weight was still dropping, in spite of the fact that all of them were even then very much under weight, and this constant loss can only be attributed to consistent under-feeding.

As late as 1943 there was evidence that the Red Cross parcels and supplies were not all reaching the prisoners, a proportion was being rifled and used by the local Japanese authorities.

Early in 1944 the rice ration was increased, but this increase only lasted for about two months, and then once more the prisoners were receiving a very insufficient diet. Fortunately the timely arrival of a further supply of Red Cross parcels once more saved the situation, but again the Japanese soon held back a proportion.

After the transfer to Sham Shui Po Camp in May, 1944, beans, bran, sugar and other Red Cross supplies came in steadily and thus helped to maintain the small improvement mentioned above.

A great contribution was made to the camp rations by the steady output of excellent vegetables, lettuces, spinach, cabbages, sweet potatoes, tomatoes and sweet corn from the camp garden; for example, during March, 1944, the total weight brought into the camp from the garden was over 5,000 lb. Although this only represents a small fraction of the prisoners' requirements, it represents great effort on the part of the prisoners and reflects great credit on those who produced it in the face of the difficulties of their daily existence.

There is no variation of standard rations at different seasons.

Prisoners employed on farming, sewing, shoe repairing and doing mess work in the camps receive full workers' rations.

AMENITIES

Between 1942 and early 1944 the Japanese gave the prisoners of war a regular monthly supply of tooth powder, toilet powder, washing soap and toilet paper, together with a barely sufficient supply of tooth brushes and face towels. During the spring of 1944, however,

the Japanese informed the prisoners that the usual monthly issue would have to last three months; this reduction became just one more hardship for the prisoners, particularly as the soap (to take an example) which was issued to them was of extremely poor quality.

A canteen had been organised on business lines in 1942 in one of the camps, but although a great variety of goods was being brought in, the very rapid rise in prices soon made it impossible for the prisoners to obtain supplies in sufficient quantity to make an appreciable addition to their rations.

RECREATION

A small area was made available in the officers' camp at Sham Shui Po for an exercise ground, but its smallness precluded the possibility of playing any games except handball. As a result, voluntary P.T. classes were started for various age groups. These performed about 20 minutes' more or less strenuous exercise in the mornings.

Camp lectures were held three times a week, covering any subject that might prove of general interest.

A library of books was acquired and proved to be about the most important source of recreation.

Some time in 1943 the prisoners were informed that the Pope had donated some money, and with this the Japanese bought for the prisoners all kinds of sports gear, tennis racquets, hockey sticks, boxing gloves and many other things which were never used because they had no opportunities. Some of the balls were the only things that proved really useful, as well as a net for deck tennis or handball.

MAIL

In the earlier years the delivery of mail sent to the prisoners was fortuitous, but the position at present seems better, although far from satisfactory. There are, of course, bound to be cases where individual prisoners have not received any mail for a long time.

From February, 1943, onwards the prisoners received a daily newspaper, "The Hong Kong News," which carried full and objective reports on the progress of the war in the West.

The prisoners are generally aware of the course of events in the Far East, and the good news from all fronts has been a great morale raiser.

I.R.C.C. VISIT

THE delegate of the I.R.C.C. again visited the camps on December 22, 1944. (His last visit in August, 1944, was summarised in the January, 1945, number of "Far East.")

Conditions were reported to be much the same in December as in August, with the following exceptions:—

Sham Shui Po Camp "S"

The strength was estimated to be about 1,200, of whom 300 sick are accommodated in eight hospital barracks. They are attended by nine British doctors and numerous male nurses belonging to the nursing staff.

The library contains some 3,000 books. Owing to the shortage of fodder the farm stock has been considerably reduced.

Sham Shui Po Camp "N"

The strength was estimated to be 400, of whom some 30 are accommodated at the camp hospital. The living quarters of this camp have been considerably enlarged by the addition of several barracks.

The library contains some 1,500 books. The area of the vegetable garden has been considerably increased, but the poultry farm has been reduced to 96 chickens.

Bowen Road Military Hospital

The number of patients was estimated to be 150, of whom there are 12 tuberculosis cases, 20 eye cases, and some prisoners still suffering from war wounds. There are 60 doctors and male nurses to attend to these patients.

The library contains some 3,000 books.

The delegate also made the following general points. The main cause of sickness throughout the various camps is avitaminosis, which manifests itself mainly in the form of beri-beri, affecting in some cases the patients' sight. The camp authorities state, however, that most cases are mild and that the state of the patients' health is improving. There are several cases of infectious interocolitis which have been isolated. The delegate believes the state of health has somewhat improved generally since the last visit, and is given to understand that the death rate continues to be low.

The monthly parcel service has been maintained without interruption. All the camps receive copies of the local newspaper edited in English. The general maintenance of the camps gave an excellent impression.

There was, however, still a great need for supplementary protein foods, fats and vitamins, particularly group "B." Facilities for supplying relief have been granted to the I.R.C.C.

Conditions in Hong Kong, January 1942 – July 1944 (from the May 1945 issue of the Far East Special Monthly Edition of *The Prisoner of War* published by the Prisoner of War Department of the Red Cross and St. John War Organization) *[21]*. Note however some of the reports in the "Far East" were unrealistic, due to various reasons, when compared with first-hand accounts such as that of Heywood.

Chapter 9

Diversions

"When all night long a chap remains
On sentry-go, to chase monotony,
He exercises of his brains,
That is presuming that he's got any."
– W.S. Gilbert

Wherever an Englishman goes, he likes to make a garden. Now that we were left more or less in peace, nearly everyone annexed a little plot somewhere or other, and whiled away many hours tilling it or talking gardening shop with his friends. The camp was transfigured; where once was bare earth or much-worn turf, there appeared neat little vegetable patches, and you could even stand in the shade of papaya or banana trees which had been grown from seed since we came into camp.

By the summer of 1944 I had regained sufficient strength to start my own garden in a vacant patch near our hut. The soil was terrible – pure red decomposed granite, which caked hard when wet. We had to dig it out to a depth of eighteen inches or more, and mix in anything we could find in the way of vegetable rubbish. Of course the great thing was to procure some manure, but the output of the camp was all supposed to go to the main camp garden … really, there was <u>nothing</u> you could call your own in this place! However, by the exercise of a little stealth and ingenuity, things could be managed; people would be dimly seen carrying malodorous buckets about under cover of darkness, and a few months later they would be boasting about their marvellous tomato crop.

I derived a lot of pleasure and a lot of sustenance from my garden; tomatoes, sweet potatoes, carrots and Chinese cabbage gave the best results, but some enterprising gardeners went in for such things as maize, ground nuts and papayas. A few strawberries were even grown in camp. Not many flowers were cultivated.

Our evenings were occasionally brightened by shows and concerts given in the theatre hut to packed audiences, who sat on the floor or on home-made stools. Some wonderful stage-settings were constructed; spectacular scenery, lighting effects and dresses were somehow improvised from make-shift materials by Sergeant-Major Baptista and his attendant wizards. Freddie Inving conducted a lively theatre orchestra; every musical show involved many hours of hard work, harmonising remembered airs and copying out scores. The acting itself, however, seldom reached the high standard of the rest of the production, partly owing to the difficulty of obtaining the books of plays. Many of us grew very tired of the succession of variety shows, with the usual risqué jokes, lack of plot, and chorus of sloppy female impersonators. The Japs who came to watch must have thought these efforts very undignified. If anyone suggested that something better might be done, the reply was that the troops would not stand any high-brow stuff – which was an undeserved slight on the intelligence of the troops. The most unlikely people developed a taste for good literature during their imprisonment, so why not for good acting and music?

Some of the orchestral concerts, however, were well worth hearing, particularly those organised by Dr. Bard.

The Japs never interfered with religious observances, and two huts were fitted up as Protestant and Roman Catholic churches respectively. One of the leading figures in camp was Padre Strong, a naval chaplain, who in his early days had served in the Merchant Marine. He knew about life and human nature as well as theology, and his forceful sermons were full of common sense. If he was depressed, he never showed it, and many of us will remember his cheerful encouragement when we were sick or depressed.

Heywood's sketch of a chapel in the camp

Sports gear had been sent into the camp from time to time, but few of us had much energy to spare for games. There were occasional cricket and hockey matches; bowls were popular, and the more energetic youngsters played volleyball. Of indoor games, bridge and chess provided as good a way as any of killing time.

Prisoners in the olden days seem to have been in the habit of carving model ships in bone, and setting them up inside bottles ... how, I do not know. We did not go in for this pastime, perhaps because the only bones available were fish bones, but some very fine ship models constructed from various materials, were shown at an Art Exhibition held in camp.

Also on show were carvings and plaques in wood, metal and slate, fancy pieces of knitting and tapestry, drawings and painting, portraits and cartoons.

Mails at first were non-existent. I did not hear from home until September, 1942 – nine months after I had been captured – and this letter was one of the very first to reach Sham Shui Po from England. The lack of communications must have been far more trying for our people at home than it was for us; many months went by before they heard whether we were alive or dead, and a year or more before letters began to arrive. We were allowed to write once every six weeks, but many of these letters and postcards never reached their destination.

We at our end fared rather better; letters from home began to trickle in with increasing frequency, though they could not say much in twenty-five words, but it was a tremendous joy to hear that they were alive and well. A few loving words from those at home upheld us when all else seemed to be failing.

Some of us, to our huge delight, even received photographs. These would be proudly shown round the hut, for admiring comments, then treasured in a pocket book or framed and hung up over one's bed.

Once or twice it was announced that a limited number of wireless messages could be sent home by prisoners in camp. I was lucky in the draw, and sent off a long message; it never reached its destination.

On one of these occasions a party leader was instructed to arrange for one of his party to send a message. He consulted his men, and after much discussion it was decided that three, who complained that they had never received letters from home, should draw lots for the privilege.

"Whom do you want to write to?" asked the party leader of the winner.

"My sister," he replied.

"Name and address?"

"Dunno 'er name now: yer see, last I 'eard of 'er she'd got married, and I've forgotten the name of the feller."

"Any idea where she lives?"

"Can't rightly say."

"Well, you must know <u>something</u> about her; when did you last see her?"

"Reckon it must be fifteen years ago!"

So he is eliminated. The second of the lucky three was a Dutchman, who wanted to send a message to Java. So the party leader trekked off to the camp office to find out if this were possible. No; messages could be sent to the British Empire only.

The third man borrowed a pencil and paper, and disappeared with a worried look on his face. After an hour he came back, and submitted his paper to the party leader.

"But you've only written about twenty words," said the latter. "You know you can send a hundred?"

"Can't think of anything else to say."

"Give it me then, and I'll see if it can be sent."

Off went the long-suffering party leader to the camp office again. Could this short message be sent? No; messages must be a hundred words long, neither more nor less.

So he returned to the hut, and offered to write out a message for the man, who shook his head and went off grumbling that he wasn't going to have any blank officers writing his blank letters for him. The party leader gave it up as a bad job, and no message was sent by the men of his group.

Books were a great standby for leisure hours. An excellent library was gradually built up with books taken from various club libraries in the town, supplemented later with those sent in by the Red Cross. Many of us were able to do more reading than ever in our lives before, and we could feel that in this respect at any rate we were not wasting our time.

Classes and lectures unfortunately were banned by the Japanese. The suspicious little blighters apparently feared that any huddle of prisoners must be plotting mutiny or escape. They could not prevent us, however, from gathering in twos or threes for study or discussion. During my stay, I learned German, studied all sorts of subjects from botany to psychology, and rubbed up my mathematics and astronomy. This all sounds rather earnest; for lighter reading I got through over two hundred novels, travel books and biographies.

The literature which came into camp with the Canadian Red Cross supplies was mostly of American origin. In addition to textbooks, there were numbers of excellent novels which gave us a valuable insight into American life from the days of the early Colonists down to the present time. We came to have very friendly feeling towards vigorous characters like Rob Ashton, Scarlet O'Hara, Babbitt and Dodsworth, who peopled these books.

If you were of an inquiring turn of mind, here was a golden opportunity of picking up all sorts of curious knowledge. Herded together in the camp were men from many different walks of life, who had had all kinds of interesting experiences and held the most divergent opinions. And it was so much easier than in peace time to make contacts with people; all you had to do was to stroll across to their hut of an evening, and sit down for a chat. They hadn't any social engagements, and they weren't in a hurry. "Hullo there! What is it you want to know? Sorry I can't offer you a drink, but sit down on my bed, and I'll tell you all about it."

A merchant skipper would tell you thrilling yarns of the China Coast; an electrical engineer would explain the fascinating workings of a big power station; and unassuming schoolmaster, once Senior Wrangler at Cambridge, would give you lessons in elementary calculus; or an R.A.F. officer would tell you of his experiences on a record-breaking long-distance flight.

On those dark evenings when no lights were allowed, many of us turned our eyes to the heavens, and began to learn something of astronomy. A group of us used to spend the evenings on a quiet bench by the bowling green, away from the crowds strolling up and down the main road or lounging outside the huts. We watched the glow of sunset fading behind Lantau, and picked out the constellations as they began to twinkle in the warm darkness, while Hesperus, serene above the western horizon, shone impartially upon captors and captives alike.

Contact with other men's minds, whether through books or at first-hand, would open up profitable lines of thought. There was plenty of time for contemplation, and many a prisoner, I think, especially if inclined towards introspection, must have reviewed his scale of values, inwardly setting his house in order, and ridding the recesses of his mind of a lot of unnecessary clutter.

Some, became cynical, for the world was in a mess, and things had gone awry with them. They began to lose their faith in human nature. "Yes", they would say, "just look at this camp! '----- you, Jack, I'm all right' is the motto here; it's each for himself and devil take the hindmost." Hunger does no doubt tend to make men selfish, and the chaos of war results in a lowering moral standards. And yet, and yet, time and again I marveled at the fundamental kindliness of my comrades; they gave away odds and ends of food and smokes and clothing to their pals, which they could ill afford; they were so willing to help in all the dull little jobs which had to be done; they refused to be depressed.

No, I didn't lose faith in human nature, but I changed my ideas about a lot of other things. Life was going by so quickly; such a big chunk of it was being wasted in prison; how should we make the best of what was left to us when we were liberated? This was a kind of chrysalis stage in our lives ... a period of inactivity during which mysterious changes where going on in our mental make-up. We could hardly expect that anything so attractive as a butterfly could ultimately emerge and flit happily away, but we could at least hope that we should be wiser and better men when we rejoined the busy world outside.

To begin with, we were gaining plenty of experience in the art of living with other people. It did not do to be fussy or irritable in an overcrowded hut; patience and forbearance were needed. Perhaps in the future we should be easier to get on with than we had been in the past.

Then again, we were not going to ask too much of life. When the war was over, we told ourselves, we would never again sigh for the moon. We had discovered that we could do perfectly well without luxuries, and we could be content with the simple things of life ... good food, decent living conditions, and the companionship of our families. We began to realize that happiness depended very little on material possessions; the loss of all our worldly goods counted for nothing compared with the loss of freedom, home life and useful employment. Life had been getting too complicated; we would surely be more grateful for the simple things. Yes, it would indeed be glorious to be free again, although perhaps we should find that work and responsibility were something of a strain after such prolonged inactivity.

It did not do to take too much thought for the morrow; better to try to live a good life each day for its own sake, and not for any vague rewards in some future existence ... anyway rather an unworthy motive, I had always thought. There was a meaning to life, here and now, ... "love thy neighbour as thyself" ... and there was one stronghold sure which would not fail me, the love of dear ones waiting for me at home. Perhaps we were unlucky to be born into this era of upheaval; perhaps though, our generation would have outstanding opportunities of shaping a better world.

Chapter 10

Trading

"Money shall make the mare to go." – Old round

Continuing the story of our hum-drum life in Sham Shui Po, Christmas came round again ... three years since the surrender, and my fourth Christmas in captivity. Peace and goodwill were a long time coming to men, and it was becoming a little difficult to greet your friends appropriately. "Happy Christmas!" was rather fatuous, for you knew quite well that it was not going to be particularly happy. "I hope you'll have a <u>really</u> happy Christmas next time" was little better, for you had said exactly the same every year, and your hopes had always failed to materialise.

All the same, this Christmas was the happiest I had spent in camp. The Christmas spirit seemed to have found its way into our hut, undeterred by its general air of bleakness and discomfort. About half of its occupants had received small parcels from friends and relatives in the town; they pooled most of these treasured gifts, and on Christmas morning divided the pool out among those of us who had not been lucky. We each received a little packet containing bananas, a few biscuits, a handful of sweets, and so on. It was a complete surprise, and such a charming gesture that I was not the only one who felt a bit lumpy in the throat.

A pig had been killed in the camp farm, and a luscious thick pork stew was served for lunch. Never did pork taste so good, but alas, many stomachs, unused to fat, subsequently rebelled. For once we ate together, at a long table decorated with flowers, and afterwards we sat round singing.

In the evening I was invited by Gerald Goodban and John Monks, two schoolmaster friends of mine, to join them and Padre Strong in sampling some home-made "hoosh". This remarkable drink had been concocted from tinned pineapples, fermented with sugar and raisins; the resulting brew was laced with a little absolute alcohol, scrounged by Gerald while out on a working party at the oil depot at Lai Chi Kok. We sat around a little dubbin-burning lamp and solemnly sampled the hoosh; it had an interesting taste, and there was certainly a kick to it. So Christmas evening was quite a festive one, and I went to bed with a pleasant glow in my inside. The pork did not trouble me, either.

Conditions in Shamshuipo

Some information has become available of conditions in this Prisoner of War Camp at Kowloon, Hong Kong, at the end of 1944

THE camp is divided into two distinct sections—the North Camp, in which are interned the prisoners of war, mainly officers, who were transferred from Argyle Street, and the South Camp which, though apparently not intended to be an "other ranks" camp, contains only a small proportion of officers. The majority of Canadian officers are in the Southern Camp.

The quarters in the Northern Camp are said to be slightly better than those in the Southern, but in other respects the conditions are similar, both camps being directly under the same Japanese officials. Internal arrangements probably vary between the two compounds as no communication is allowed between the two senior British officers.

Rations, which are generally inadequate, include fish, vegetables, rice, a little sugar, salt, soya beans and nuts. No tea, coffee, cocoa, milk, eggs or butter are ever issued. Prisoners of war do their own cooking and eat in their barracks. All have knives, forks and containers. There should officially be three meals each day, but often the shortage of food is such that only two meals can be taken.

It is thought that the prisoners have mosquito nets. The men have iron bedsteads, but there is a shortage of bedding. Some have enough to wear, but the majority do not.

An aerial photograph of Hong Kong, taken before the war.

and there is a considerable shortage of shoes and boots, most prisoners of war going about barefooted.

Working parties go out from the camp each day—usually by truck—and the men receive a very little pay. Religious services are held in both camps.

Care of the Sick

The medical care of the prisoners of war is, for the most part, in the hands of British medical officers. A Japanese doctor visits the camp monthly for the purpose of examining the prisoners of war and reporting on their health. This examination is generally very casual. In an epidemic, the sick are removed to hospital and the remainder inoculated.

There is a cemetery situated near the former officers' camp in Kowloon, in which the bodies of prisoners of war who have died in Shamshuipo camp are interred. The graves are marked by a stone bearing a number, and friends are allowed to attend the funeral.

Some prisoners receive private parcels from friends outside the camp, and there have been issues of Red Cross parcels. The parcels are examined by the Japanese and distributed by representatives of the prisoners of war under supervision by the Japanese.

Conditions in Sham Shui Po (from the August 1945 issue of the Far East Special Monthly Edition of *The Prisoner of War* published by the Prisoner of War Department of the Red Cross and St. John War Organization) *[22]*

Air raids over Hong Kong were now becoming more frequent and intensive, no doubt in connection with the great allied drive through the Philippines and northward, towards Japan. A tremendous raid took place on January 16th, 1945, lasting most of the day. Again and again the American fighters and bombers made low-flying attacks on the shipping in the harbour; they took our breath away with their gallantry, and several of them, alas, were brought down. The attackers evidently knew the position of the prison camp, and no bombs fell in or near it, although more than once we heard the ominous rush preceding the explosion. A number of beastly little pom-pom shells, however, fell within the fence and exploded on contact, not to mention a shower of shell splinters. Fortunately there were no casualties. The racket was tremendous, and it was a very wearing day.

A week or two later I was on a working party at Lai Chi Kok. We were cleaning empty oil drums in a big shed, a process which made as much noise as the unloading of a milk train. Suddenly, I became aware that everybody was running away, so I ran, too. Apparently the air raid warning had sounded, and nobody in the shed had heard it. We were still running when the bombs fell on the far side of the harbour, and the whole show was over by the time we had reached the shelter. This was the occasion when a formation came over at a great height, and bombed the Naval yard at Wanchai.

I was now going out on working parties every ten days or so. I did not enjoy them particularly, but at any rate the workers were rewarded with a little extra food. I spent one amusing morning in the welding shop at Lai Chi Kok, acting as assistant to a little Jap welder, who was mending holes in oil drums. Part of my job was to trundle up a damaged drum, and hold it steady for him while he worked. He would first test the drum for petrol vapour by the simple method of applying his oxy-acetylene flame to the open filler-hole. A number of drums had been repaired without any untoward incident, and I had just rolled up a fresh one and was leaning on it to keep it steady. The welder applied his flame to the hole. Woosh! The drum shot off like a flying rocket to the other side of the shed, leaving me sprawling. After that, I noticed that the welder sniffed cautiously at each drum before trying any experiments with the flame.

February was a beastly month, cold, wet and dreary. A big working party was sent away to do gardening at Happy Valley, on the Island, spending the nights at Bowen Road Hospital. They were badly overworked; all lost weight and were run down. It was pathetic to see their delight at getting back "home" to Sham Shui Po. They must have indeed had a bad time if they could look forward with pleasure to their return to this unattractive camp.

We were all much cheered by an announcement in the paper that a relief ship would shortly bring Red Cross supplies for British and American prisoners in China and the southern regions. For weeks this was the one topic of conversation in camp, and the wildest rumours and speculations ran around as to the amount and contents of the parcels, Alas for high hopes! When, after maddening delays, the consignment arrived in camp, it was much smaller than we had expected, and was found to consist of very bedraggled-looking bales of three-year-old parcels.

News went round that there would be less than two parcels per man. Now each parcel was intended by the senders to last one prisoner for a month; hitherto, during three years, we had received exactly six and two-thirds parcels per man! And we knew very well that this was not the fault of our people at home.

Our spirits collapsed like a pricked balloon; we were just like children whose eagerly-awaited presents have failed to come up their expectations. But we were considerably cheered when we came to open our parcels, for, despite their battered exteriors, their contents were in excellent condition ... a tribute to British war-time production. Even the chocolate was delicious, though it had not been packed for the tropics.

The consignment also included clothing, toilet kits and so on, which were distributed amongst us. A large number of personal parcels, containing smokes and comforts, arrived for the Canadians, who were most generous in handing out cigarettes.

We were now well off for kit, for we had already received various issues of clothing from previous Red Cross consignments. The cold weather was over and we did not expect to be prisoners for another winter, so naturally we wished to trade our kit for food; after all, we could get through the summer in any old rags, and we didn't want to starve. Now our sentries at that time were Formosans – only the officers, interpreters and N.C.O.'s being Japanese. The former had no love for the Japs, and paid little respect to the rules and regulations of the Japanese army; in fact it was said that they gave the authorities a good deal more trouble than did the prisoners themselves.

The sentries could speak Cantonese, and made contacts in the town, where clothing and other commodities fetched fantastic prices. And so the great Trading Racket began. Within the camp various individuals, with sound commercial instincts, set up as middlemen between the sentries and the prisoners. Nobody grudged them a reasonable profit on their transactions, for they were performing a useful service in procuring a large amount of food-stuffs for the hungry camp, and underselling the now almost useless canteen. Besides, they took the risk of a beating-up, for the whole business was entirely against the rules.

So if you were the possessor of a brand-new blanket, or a nice pair of Canadian gauntlet gloves, or a pullover lovingly knitted by kind ladies at home, or anything that you thought you could dispense with, you would take it round to one of these trading gentlemen. A whispered colloquy would ensue, though I could never make out why such terrific secrecy was needed. The trader would promise to obtain a good cash price for you from his friends amongst the sentries, and if his terms were good you would naturally go to him when you wanted to buy food.

Prices were fantastic. The military yen, which had replaced the Hong Kong dollar, was officially quoted at 8/4d in 1943; beans now cost some 50 yen per lb., coarse brown sugar 20 yen, onions the same, duck eggs 15 yen each, a box of matches 4 yen, so the actual purchasing power of the yen was less than a farthing. Inflation was growing, and the yen took a further plunge downwards on the fall of Germany. Conditions in the town simply did not bear thinking of; rice, which in peace-time sold at about 10 cents a catty, now cost over 100 yen.

So it did not do to hold on to your cash. As soon as possible you bought food with it. Trading reached impressive proportions, for there were still over a thousand men in camp, and all of them were selling every bit of kit they could spare. Under cover of darkness, the sentries would come in laden with sacks of sugar and baskets of duck eggs; eventually they even used to employ coolies to help them bring in the goods. The traders were liable to be woken up at any time of night by a sentry anxious to do business.

Once, in the middle of the night, some brisk bargaining was going on between a sentry and a trader, while a coolie stood by with his bamboo carrying-pole and two great baskets of groceries. Suddenly a torch-light appeared at the opposite end of the hut. The sentry hopped out of the window, the coolie dived under a bed, and the trader buried himself under the blankets and pretended to be asleep. The light drew nearer, flashing from side to side of the hut; it was carried by one of the interpreters, checking the numbers to see that nobody had escaped.

He reached the trader's bed, and tripped over a basket obstructing the gangway; shining his torch around, he spotted a pair of feet sticking out from under a bed. Everybody held their breath, but instead of continuing his investigations, the Jap strolled on down the hut, passed the time of night with the picket on duty at the door, and disappeared. There were no subsequent repercussions; evidently the interpreter was getting his rake-off from the trading.

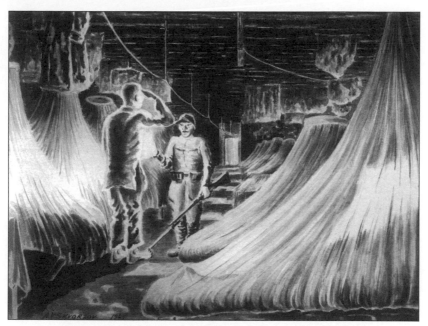

Sham Shui Po Camp night count by Lt. A.V. Skvorza *[23]*

The reader may find it difficult to believe the following incident, but it is perfectly true. Two or three months later, at the prison hospital at the Central British School, a sentry wished to take out a large bundle of clothing to sell in the town for one of the patients, who had set up as a trader. The trader demanded cash for the goods. "No have got" said the sentry. They argued for a long time, the trader insisting that the sentry must leave some security if he could not pay cash down.

The sentry scratched his head, eventually broke into a beaming smile, and said, "I know, master; I leave you my rifle; you keep till I come back tomorrow night with the money!" So the trader hid the rifle under his mattress for the next twenty-four hours; had there been a search, its presence might have been difficult to explain!

Bowen Road Hospital was closed down in March, 1945, and the patients and staff transferred for a few weeks to Sham Shui Po, until new quarters were ready for them at the Central British School at Kowloon.

The officers from Argyle Street had also been moved into Sham Shui Po some time before; they occupied the northern part of the camp, which was now separated from us by a double line of fence with a no-man's-land of empty huts between. The arrival of the hospital inmates involved some re-shuffling of huts; the fences between the two camps were shifted, and the resulting confusion provided a golden opportunity of slipping across the boundary and chatting with friends. Crowds of people hob-nobbed in no-man's-land, until a shout would warn them that a sentry was approaching, when everybody would scatter wildly in opposite directions. I had a long talk with John Barrow, a great friend of mine whom I had not seen for three years.

That evening a fierce detail was issued, stating that anyone communicating in any way with the officers' camp would be shot.

One morning, about a week later, I was suddenly warned to be ready to leave camp in an hour and a half. My master was being transferred to the new hospital, and I was to go as his attendant. It was a wrench leaving my beloved little garden just as the potatoes were coming on nicely, but we were glad enough when the gates shut behind us and we waved good-bye to Sham Shui Po … as we hoped, forever. It seems that my departure was observed by Chungking agents in the town, for a report reached England that I had been sent away to Japan. This caused much needless anxiety to my relatives.

The Central British School was positively luxurious; I suppose the Japs saw the end of the war approaching, and wished to make a good show with their prison hospital when Hong Kong returned to its rightful owners. The building was modern, well-designed, and completely undamaged by the war. It stood on a hill, wide open to the breeze and commanding lovely views on both sides. The wards, which once had been class-rooms, were clean airy, and free from bugs. The windows opened and shut properly, and were fitted with real glass … delightful novelty! Along each side ran shady verandahs, where there was room for comfortable chairs. The sanitary arrangements were civilised.

Oh, the joy of getting into bed that night … a real bed, with a spring frame and soft mattress, cool sheets and a voluptuous pillow. Truly bed is one of man's greatest inventions, evolved by slow degrees down the ages to its present state of perfection. Beds have brought more happiness than all your wireless sets and motor cars and aeroplanes. Most inventions seem to be misused these days, but not beds; people don't go blowing each other into smithereens with beds. I have always appreciated my bed. Beds are the thing!

This move, I thought to myself as I drowsed off, will certainly be for the better, if only the food is adequate; no bugle … we always used to wonder what new annoyance was in store for us when "Orderly Sergeants" was sounded.

We were eight in the ward … a comfortable fit without overcrowding. There were three men blinded in the war, Lieut. Thomson (eye injuries), and we four attendants. The cheerfulness and courage of those blind men made me feel very humble. They never complained of their lot. For most of us the long evenings without lights were trying enough; for them it would always be a blackout, complete and life-long. And yet it was a cheerful room … I think we made more noise than the rest of the wards put together.

In all there were rather more than a hundred patients in the hospital. These included the prisoners permanently disabled by war wounds, and the "old men" of over sixty, who had been transferred from Sham Shui Po to more comfortable quarters here. Surely all these should have been repatriated years ago. Man of the remaining patients were recovering from severe effects of Malnutrition; some had suffered from paralysis, and were perseveringly learning to walk again, like babies taking their first steps. Fortunately, there were not many cases of dangerous illness, though now and then a very sick man would be brought from Sham Shui

Po, and occasionally the screens would go up round a bed, and a little funeral party would go out to the cemetery nearby.

Col. Bowie, of the R.A.M.C., was in charge of the hospital under the Japanese, with Major Anderson as second in command and surgeon. The latter had been one of the leading civilian doctors in Hong Kong. It was a pleasure to work under these two men after our experiences in Sham Shui Po. Ever since the capitulation they had striven to ease the lot of sick and wounded prisoners, in spite of endless obstructions put in their way by the Japanese. Thanks to them and their staff of doctors, orderlies, cooks and maintenance men, life in the hospital went as smoothly and happily as was possible in the circumstances.

The rations were distinctly better to begin with than they had been in Sham Shui Po, which reconciled me for the loss of all those lovely potatoes. We found life very quiet and uneventful – indeed at times I was bored. There was less going on, less gossip and less room for exercise, although there was a pleasant lawn on which to take the air. Before long, however, we settled down to our new routine, and I found the days slipping by quickly enough. There were the usual chores to do, German lessons with Bob Bickley (one of the blind lads), and a good deal of reading aloud. A communal garden was started, which provided the more energetic of us with as much digging exercise as we required, and surprisingly soon began to provide the hospital with vey welcome additions to the vegetable rations.

It was a joyful day when we heard of the surrender of Germany; the carnage was over at any rate on that side of the world, and our families in England would be safe from bombs and V2 rockets … whatever they might be. It was indeed heartening news, but we could not expect it to have any immediate effect on us, for few of us were optimistic enough to hope that Japan would ask for terms now that she faced the world alone.

Not long afterwards all news was stopped; we heard nothing more of events in the outside world except from an occasional rumour from a sentry. It was very trying; we felt that the end must be near, and yet the months dragged by and nothing happened. Hong Kong now seemed completely dead; in four months we saw only two vessels coming in through Lyemoon Pass, and they both appeared to be hospital ships. During this period only one air-raid took place, and Albert's visits became rarer and rarer and finally stopped altogether. The conflict seemed to have passed Hong Kong by, leaving it forgotten! The gales of war were sweeping all around us, in China, Burma, Borneo, Luzon, Okinawa, and still we waited in the calm centre of the cyclone. Every lorry humming along the road made us prick up our ears, hoping that we heard the approach of Allied aircraft; every rumble of blasting or practice artillery-fire made us wonder for a moment whether the longed-for invasion was beginning.

The rations, which had started so well, soon dwindled again, and before the end we were subsisting on the very minimum of rice and "green horror", eked out with a little bit of meat and a slice of cake once a week. The supplies of vitamin capsules and drugs from the Red Cross were almost exhausted. Most people began to lose weight again, and the outlook for the future was none too rosy. But people continued to be wildly optimistic; "Any day, now!" they would say. The invasion must be imminent.

In order to counteract undue optimism and subsequent disappointment, the occupants of our ward formed themselves into "The Grim and Glum Club". We assured each other that the war would last into 1946; heartiness was frowned on; our motto was "When everything looks grim and glum, remember there's still worse to come!!", and our theme song "A few more years shall roll".

Chapter 11

Operation Joyride

"Journeys end in lovers' meeting." – Shakespeare

August came in with beautiful days; towering white clouds drifted gently over the hills on the south wind, and we would lounge on the terrace in the afternoons basking in the blazing sunshine. Everything seemed utterly peaceful; there was no sound or movement in the town around us.

And then one day the news filtered in, and was whispered around the hospital, that Russia had invaded Manchuria. We heard nothing more until Thursday, August 16th. This was a very curious day, in the morning the Japs were observed to be burning their documents in the incinerator … the first sign of changes to come. Rumours were circulated of a landing at Osaka, then that fighting had ceased. A sentry coming from Sham Shui Po in the evening informed us that the band had been playing and the prisoners making merry all day. Another said "you very happy; I too very happy; soon go back to my house in Formosa." But evening muster took place as usual; Capt. Saito, the Japanese medical officer in charge of the hospital, was in a vile temper, and refused to say a word.

What was really happening? Was Hong Kong to be handed back without the horrors of another invasion? Was this only an armistice, or had Japan surrendered? There were some very sick men in hospital, who could be saved by good food, and for their sake particularly we trusted that the rumours were not false. We could hardly believe that our three-and-a-half years of imprisonment were really ending; the whole atmosphere was so completely vague and quiet and undramatic. We went to bed in a mood of subdued optimism, but bubbling with impatience to see the outcome of the next few days.

At breakfast the following morning I was so far convinced that the end was at hand, that I unearthed my "siege rations", and distributed some of them around the ward. These consisted of a tin of powdered milk, a small tin of biscuits, and a tin of bully beef, which I had set aside from my Red Cross parcels in case the food supply failed during the hope-for invasion, or I had been forced to try to escape. It had needed considerable self-control to refrain from eating them during the last few hungry months; I had kept them at the bottom of my kit-bag, stuffed all my winter clothes on top of them, shut up the kit-bag in a cupboard, and tried to forget about it.

This day, August 17th, also passed quietly. It was rumoured that a relief convoy was on its way to Hong Kong. Time and again we looked towards Lyemoon Pass, but the water lay blue and still, and no ships appeared. A big Union Jack was taken from its place of concealment, and made ready for hoisting. That was most heartening, for never since we had been captured had we been allowed to keep Union Jacks (much less fly them), or to sing the National Anthem. A wag went round hospital shouting "Upper berth for you, cabin number so and so, D. deck! … Yes, sir? Would you like to sit at the captain's table?"

During the day two strangers were brought into hospital, with no belongings save the clothes they stood up in. They turned out to be American spies, who had penetrated into occupied China from Yunnan a year previously, and had been captured about a month ago. Miraculously they had not been executed. We did not care to press them for details of their story, for they were obviously weary, but we gathered a little news about the outside world. Evidently it was a great mercy that Hong Kong had been spared another invasion, for they told us that the place was strongly fortified and that the Americans were prepared to launch an overwhelming attack on it. Our position would have been a most uncomfortable one.

That evening there was no muster for the first time for years. And lights were allowed; a lighted room looked strange and unreal after groping around after dark for so many months. We held an impromptu sing-song in the school hall, which enabled us to blow off some of our suppressed excitement in cheerful noise.

Nobody in our ward thought of going to bed. We were chatting on the verandah, when we heard a call from the barbed wire fence on the far side of the drive. One of us climbed over the parapet and walked across the road to investigate; a few seconds later he came running back out of the shadows with another figure, small and active, who he helped on to the verandah. She slipped into our ward to be out of sight of any prying Japs, and started asking after various friends in the hospital and camp. She was an internee from a nearby camp, and finding that restrictions were relaxed she had very pluckily slipped across the fields to visit us.

Our visitor disappeared again into the night, and we noticed that the Japanese guard were also departing with all their belongings. Saito was still with us. He was taking things with very bad grace; in spite of repeated requests by the Colonel, he had refused to give us a word of information, and now we could hear him smashing windows in his quarters in the far wing of the building. Some of us slipped out into the garden and armed ourselves with picks and spades, in case he turned nasty. At last, at about midnight, he walked away down the drive, looking neither to right nor left, with his sword drawn and his left hand on the butt of his revolver.

So we were left, no longer hemmed in by armed men, once more under the command of our own officers. It was a queer situation, and an uneasy one. Two or three thousand British ex-prisoners and internees were scattered about Hong Kong in the various camps, unarmed and physically in poor shape. The Japs were still in charge of the Colony, and responsible for law and order. Presumably their country had surrendered, but they had not yet given up their arms; no doubt they were in a bitter mood. And there was a huge Chinese population, all hating the Japs, many starving and ready to take desperate measures to obtain food. We set a guard on the hospital, and longed more fervently than ever for the arrival of allied warships.

No one could sleep; the lights remained on in most of the wards, and people sat up talking. The orderlies raided the Japs' garden for sweet potatoes. In the small hours of the morning there was a heavy shower, and as it cleared the setting moon threw a pale silvery lunar rainbow over Kowloon Bay. It seemed a good omen.

August 18th. All who could leave their beds fell in at 7.30 a.m. on the drive in front of the verandah. The Colonel called us to attention, and we saluted as the Union Jack was slowly hoisted. A chord was sounded on a piano inside the building; we sang "God save the King", but our voices were shaky; it was a very great moment.

During the morning the more energetic of us experimented with our new-found freedom. I walked out through the gates as bold as you please, strolled down the hill and along the road, nodding affably to any Chinese or Indians who looked friendly, and cutting any Japs dead. It was very strange, and I wished my legs felt as lively as my spirits.

I visited some Eurasian friends of mine, who told me something of the heartrending experiences of those who had remained at large in the town. The Japanese rule had been a grim and a terrible one.

Back to hospital for lunch. Plenty of food was now coming in, and we could stuff ourselves to repletion at every meal … a delightful experience. There was a constant stream of visitors to the hospital throughout the day; old friends, some of them sadly aged in appearance, were greeting one another. Everybody was swapping experiences, or retailing news and rumours. A party from Sham Shui Po told how the flag had been hoisted there, how Honda had been cheered and the Fat Pig booed, and how our Liaison Officer and some of his satellites had been put under arrest.

Some American fighter planes came over in the afternoon and dropped leaflets. From these we learned authentically for the first time that Japan had capitulated; the Japs were to remain in charge until allied forces arrived to take over, and meanwhile a Red Cross representative was on his way. It was rather a formal and chilling message; it did not even say "It won't be long now!". When would those ships turn up?

During the next few days we began to realise that we should have to wait patiently a little longer; vast numbers of prisoners and internees were scattered all over the Far East, and we could not all be sorted out in a week or two. In order to avoid any unfortunate incidents in the town, the Colonel issued orders that no one was to wander without leave beyond the immediate vicinity of the hospital. A couple of Japs appeared with a message from the Governor of Hong Kong politely requesting us to refrain from flying the Union Jack; it could be seen from many parts of the town, and might incite the Chinese to make trouble. The latter had been forbidden to fly Chungking flags. We compromised by saying that our flag would in any case be lowered at sundown, and we would not fly it on the morrow. So nobody lost face.

And still no allied warship appeared in Lyemoon Bay.

The time passed quickly enough for me, for I was put on to a full-time job as an orderly in an officers' ward. Here, late one evening, we received a draft of about twenty "convicts" from Canton. These were the survivors of a number of Hong Kong prisoners and internees who had been convicted of communicating with the Allies, attempting to escape, and so on. A few had been executed, some had died in Stanley gaol; the remainder had been transferred to a military prison in Canton, where they were serving long terms of imprisonment when the war came to an end. Only the previous day they had been taken from their cells and sent by train to join us at Hong Kong.

With their shaven heads and pale faces they looked in worse shape than we. But most of them were fairly fit … certainly no thinner than the rest of us … for their rations seem to have been rather better than ours. The mental stain must have been severe; every day they had to sit for long hours facing the blank wall of their cell; if they moved or spoke, they risked a beating from the sentry who prowled around the prison in stockinged feet, peeping in at each cell as he passed. They were allowed out for ten minutes' P.T. daily.

The Chinese and Jap prisoners there fared even worse; so strict was the discipline that, when out on working parties, they even had to ask permission to wipe the sweat off their brows!

The British party came out undefeated and undismayed by their long ordeal. They were talkative and cheerful, and touchingly grateful for any help we could give them.

Theirs was not the only story of courage and endurance we heard. Amongst the visitors to the hospital were many of the brave people who had remained loyal in the town, refusing to take jobs under the Japs, and endeavouring to help prisoners and internees in various ways. They were under suspicion, and lived in constant fear lest one day the Gestapo car would "pick them up" with no word of explanation. They somehow managed to exist by selling their valuables bit by bit. When Hong Kong returns to normal, I hope these citizens will not be forgotten.

It dawned on us that our stay in Sham Shui Po had been a picnic compared with life in the town or in the Canton gaol.

We were greatly cheered when, on August 29th, British planes showing the markings of the Fleet Air Arm came roaring over the hospital, diving, zooming and waggling their wings. Staff and up-patients crowded the roof and tower, to wave and shout in reply. Clearly the Fleet was near.

Bored with uncertainty, I felt like taking a holiday, so put myself down for one of the organised parties which were being taken over daily to Stanley camp. The following morning I started on my jaunt, joining a large party from Sham Shui Po. We crossed in a ferry, and as our buses laboured up the hill to Wong Nei Cheong Gap, we looked back across the harbour, and saw ... joyful sight ... a British destroyer steaming slowly in, followed by a cruiser. They had come at last, and all the doubts of the last fortnight were over.

I spent a delightful day at Stanley, greeted by many old friends. Among them was Evans, who had given us up for lost that evening three and a half years ago, when Starbuck and I had failed to return from Au Tau.

Accounts of life in the internment camp differed widely. One friend, an enthusiastic biologist, was full of his doings; he had grown champion vegetables, had seen all sorts of rare birds (including vultures, after the corpses) and had run a successful yeast brewery. Altogether, he said, it had been a great experience ... a bit too long, perhaps, but not bad fun at all.

Another ended up her account by saying "Oh, Mr. Heywood, it was hell on earth".

It all depended on their point of view.

In the afternoon, the camp was visited by Admiral Harcourt, the C. in C. of the relieving squadron, who had made it his business to see all the prisoners and internees as soon as he landed. The Union Jack and allied flags were hoisted, and fluttered gaily in the dazzling sunshine, while the Admiral spoke to the assembled internees. He explained why the taking over of Hong Kong had been delayed; the war in the Far East had come to an end unexpectedly soon, and his squadron had steamed at full speed all the way from Sydney to relieve us.

It was time to go. A jolly crowd of friends saw us off. People were happy once more; we were coming back to life. Darkness had fallen by the time we had reached the city; the Japs were still in charge, and their sentries

Raising of the Union Jack on 30 August 1945 at Stanley Internment Camp [24]

Liberated Canadian POWs at Sham Shui Po camp in August 1945 [25]

stood at the street corner glaring nervously from side to side, their bayonets at the ready, their backs against the walls. They were in for an uncomfortable night.

Our buses were diverted into the naval yard, which had just been taken over by landing parties from the ships. Armed blue-jackets were everywhere; to us they looked simply enormous; their chests were huge, their muscles bulged, and they towered over the Chinese crowding round the gate. No wonder they looked gigantic – they were almost the first well-fed men we had seen.

They were so kind; they welcomed us, entertained us as best they could in the chaos left by the Japs, and finally packed us all off, sleepy and content, in a big motor boat to Sham Shui Po.

Things began to move. The next day the sick prisoners were taken on board a hospital ship; more warships and transports arrived; troops reinforced the naval landing parties. We began to hear stirring tales of the war;

we learned of the bewildering technical advances which had been made; we were four years out of date ... back numbers. It was a strange and rather intimidating world into which we were emerging from chrysalises.

Sham Shui Po Camp after liberation *[26]*

A few days later I left the now empty hospital to resume duty at the Observatory. Any essential-service men who were reasonably fit came back from the camps to their old jobs for a while, until the military administration was fully established.

The three of us – Evans, Starbuck and myself, strolled up the shady drive to the old place, and peered around our old haunts, remembering former days. The offices and rooms were in a mess, our household belongings were gone, weeds and creepers rioted over the gardens, but the buildings were undamaged, and the compound was cool and green and peaceful as of old.

It was the day on which Kowloon was re-occupied, and a guard of Marines arrived to take over from the handful of Japs who were stationed at the Observatory. We had the pleasure of watching the little men being politely but very firmly rounded up. A heavy shower had come on, and they were marched away, bent under their heavy packs, dripping and dismal. The circle of events was complete; the usurpers had gone, and we were back once more where we belonged.

There is little more to tell. The Navy people were unendingly kind and helpful; and our duties at the Observatory were not too strenuous.

Sham Shui Po Camp in September 1945 *[27]*

We salvaged what little of the equipment had been left by the Japs, and restrained some over-enthusiastic souvenir-hunters among the guard. We got into touch with some of the survivors of the Chinese staff. In conjunction with the Naval meteorologists, the typhoon warning service was re-organised. The rest would have to wait until new equipment was obtained.

We were quartered in great luxury at the Peninsula Hotel from which we were allowed to send a free cable home. To our unbounded joy, the replies came back within a few days; our families seemed much less remote.

On September 18th I embarked on H.M.S. "Glengyle", and sailed for home with a party of 150 internees from Stanley. It was an unforgettable trip; the ship's company called it "Operation Joyride", and did everything in their power to make it so. They let us swarm over the ship, and fed us sumptuously in relays in the wardroom, they entertained us with songs and talks and cinema shows, and they played with the children. Good food worked wonders, and we put on weight at an alarming speed. And it was even more of a tonic, after the lifeless years of

The Hong Kong Observatory in the early 1950s

Tsim Sha Tsui and Victoria Harbour viewed from the Observatory in 1948
[28]

Views from the Observatory in the early 1950s

The Peninsula Hotel in Tsim Sha Tsui, still in camouflage colours, shortly after the re-occupation of Hong Kong by British forces *[29]*

futility, to be among men who had undertaken a great task, and had gloriously succeeded. And although they had been at war for years, they had not become dulled and cynical; they were still full of kindliness and gaiety. It was a happy ship.

At Colombo we bade them goodbye regretfully, and trans-shipped to the "Maloja", a big P. & O. trooper. We went ashore at Suez, to be fitted out at the big clothing depot there; it was wonderfully organised, but time did not allow us to choose very well-fitting clothes.

HMS Glengyle *[30]*

P. & O. Maloja *[31]*

At Port Said I received a cable from my wife telling me to look out for a bunch of yellow chrysanthemums on the quay at Southampton. I had not seen England for nearly nine years; it looked as green and lovely as ever as we steamed up Southampton Water on a sunny October afternoon.

The ship drew slowly into the docks, listing heavily with the weight of thousands of men crowding the rail. I strained my eyes towards the small cluster of people on the quay; yes, sure enough, there was a speck of yellow, and soon I could see a well-loved figure holding the chrysanthemums. Our dreams had come true.

*** The End ***

Mrs Heywood at the Kowloon Welfare Centre of the HKSPC at Portland Street, Mong Kok

MUMMY'S BANYAN TREE

A recollection of my parents, by Veronica Heywood

My father was a scientist, a meteorologist, an astronomer and a very keen amateur botanist and ornithologist. He spent his career as the Director of the Royal Observatory, Hong Kong. He loved rambling through the hills and valleys of the Hong Kong countryside with his family and friends. In 1935 he published a book called *Rambles in Hong Kong*. My beloved Dad died in 1985.

My mother, while enthusiastically accompanying my father on his expeditions, had her own vital work to do. Hong Kong has had a long history of nurturing people who seek asylum. My mother helped run the Kowloon Welfare Centre of the Hong Kong Society for the Protection of Children (HKSPC), turning nobody away. She appealed for food, clothes and equipment; she found out what their trades had been; if they had been in the rag trade she would find them a sewing machine, or if they had been carpenters she'd find their suitable tools. I remember hearing Mum making an appeal over Radio Hong Kong and thinking at the time that she sounded very appealing!

Hong Kong at that time was just a busy trading port; my darling Mum, without realising, might have been partly responsible for turning Hong Kong into the industrial beehive it is today.

Mummy died in the late summer on 17th August 1992, shortly before I started my travels. She had been suffering from Alzheimer's disease and her memory had stuck in the groove of her brain that stored not only "When I was in Hong Kong" but also, after my father's death, thinking that his absence was due to his incarceration as a POW. When I returned to Hong Kong I was able to remember her in her prime together with my father, while drawing from the deep well of my childhood subconscious.

St Andrew's, the church where my mother married my father, still stands, minus its steeple, taken down as a precaution rather than to be blown down by a typhoon, and hasn't been replaced by a multistorey skyscraper. The fading wedding photographs evoke the carefree, somewhat privileged tropical lifestyle of two handsome young people and their friends. There is no shadow of the pending holocaust that affected all their lives irrevocably.

The Heywoods' wedding at St Andrew's Church, Kowloon

The bride's copious bouquet contradicts my mother's great love of all living things; the floral bounty must have denuded several large glasshouses. I can remember when her passion bubbled over into direct action. There were plans to widen Nathan Road (the Golden Mile, where you can purchase anything you want) and to fell the avenue of giant banyan trees. These gleaming-leafed tropical trees can survive many centuries, for when their main trunk suffers from fatigue, aerial roots dropping down from their branches take over and support the tree as if with crutches. My mother reacted to this information by racing down

the drive and tying herself suffragette-like to the trunk of one of these mighty trees, in so doing drawing attention to both herself (something she'd always told us not to do) and the fate of the magnificent trees.

My mother would have been delighted to hear that her banyan trees are still providing shade and oxygen to the shoppers along the Golden Mile.

Gathering storms

The joy my parents felt in the early years of their marriage was to be short-lived. In the face of the threat of invasion by the Japanese army, families were advised to evacuate Hong Kong. My father decided to escort his wife and little daughter, Susan, safely out of danger's way to stay with friends near Melbourne, Australia. After a short leave he returned to his work in the Observatory. Susan's earliest memory was of waving and watching her

Mummy's banyan trees at the Nathan Road entrance of the Observatory *[32]*

father taking off on a grey, overcast morning from Melbourne Harbour in a flying boat.

My parents had treated their brief holiday as a second honeymoon. My mother was now expecting her second child… me. She moved to a cottage to be near the hospital in Blackrock, a suburb of Melbourne.

On 8 December 1941 Japanese forces invaded Hong Kong; my mother was seven months into her pregnancy. There was an ominous silence from her husband that lasted for many months, with no information as to whether he was alive or dead.

I had always been curious as to why my mother boarded HMS *Strathallan* for war-torn Europe just a few weeks after I was born; leaving the relative safety of Australia, crossing two oceans via the U-boat infested Panama Canal, in an unescorted, unarmed passenger liner.

I discovered the reason in a hostelry in Dublin, where I met an elderly man who had a speech defect. I thought he had a cleft palate but, listening to him carefully, he had a very different story. He was living in Darwin, Australia, when, on the morning of 19 February 1942, 242 Japanese aircraft attacked the city, killing at least 243 people and causing immense damage. The man escaped the worst of injuries but a piece of shrapnel sliced through the roof of his mouth. There must have been a feeling across the whole continent that the Japanese were planning a massive invasion. Hence my mother took the first opportunity, after my advent, to return to family and friends, thinking in doing so that if my father was still alive the family would eventually be reunited.

My mother smoothed over her harrowing journey by telling of domestic crises such as having to keep her cabin door ajar, in case of torpedo attack, while she was breast feeding me: "So embarrassing, dear, as there were soldiers walking up and down the companion ways!" It was only when a small suitcase was opened recently, to reveal drafts of letters my mother wrote to her parents and her in-laws (whom she had yet to meet), my birth certificate and a hand-drawn card celebrating my christening, that the tension my mother experienced was revealed. A penciled draft letter to her in-laws dated April 23 included the following: "There is danger everywhere now... Safety does not always mean survival... I did not want my children in Jap hands." Then in a post-script she adds: "I wonder if there's any more news of my beloved Gra? I haven't had news of any description from anyone for such ages, so I'm longing for some."

Veronica's christening spoon on board HMS *Strathallan*

Photo of Veronica with her mother; the back of the photo, addressing it to
Mr Heywood at Camp S (Sham Shui Po camp)

My christening must have been light relief from the wartime tension.
The ceremony was performed by Captain J.H. Biggs and fellow passengers
were only too willing to take up their roles as proxy Godparents. Heddle

Nash, the tenor, who was obviously returning from a concert tour of Australia, was amongst them. Eileen B. Smith, who had been evacuated from Hong Kong at the same time as my mother, was another volunteer Godparent. (Three years later, when my mother first made contact with my father after his capture, Eileen heard that her husband had been killed trying to defend Stanley in December 1941).

HMS *Strathallan*, having managed to avoid the U-boats, made a brief port of call at Derry in Northern Ireland, and docked at Glasgow. The ship has another heroic story beyond delivering the Heywood family safely home, but that is for another to tell.

My mother took the safest option: not to stay with her parents, who lived near Portsmouth, a target for German bombs, but to rely on her yet-to-be-met in-laws, whose home was near the Welsh border, far away from any city.

When Victory in Europe was declared my mother moved south to rent a cottage next door to her parents. In spite of all the upheavals, my father's Observatory salary arrived every month, saving the family from destitution.

I have a vivid memory, my first, of being taken up to the top of a hill on the Isle of Wight to watch a great fire. There was an atmosphere of both relief and excitement; much later I learnt that fires were lit on high ground all around England's coast to celebrate VJ day.

Not long after, the whole family climbed up to our grandparents' attic and peered out of a dormer window at the Solent (the shipping approach to Southampton). I couldn't see what they all were looking at with such excitement, so climbed up onto somebody's shoulders. There was a bee and I put my hand on it, letting out shrieks of pain, but I'd just caught a glance at the great, grey ship sailing slowly up the Solent.

Daddy was coming home!

SOME DRAWINGS BY GRAHAM HEYWOOD

Sketch of the Director's quarters at the Observatory (1947)

Watercolour of the Director's quarters at the Observatory (1952)

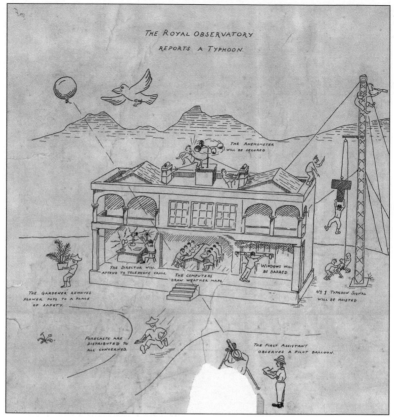

Cartoon: "The Royal Observatory reports a typhoon"

Following: Drawings from *Rambles in Hong Kong*

Waterwheel

Lan Tau Peak from the North-East

The Pat Sin Range and Plover Cove from the South

Port Shelter from Tate's Cairn

The Temple, Shatin Pass

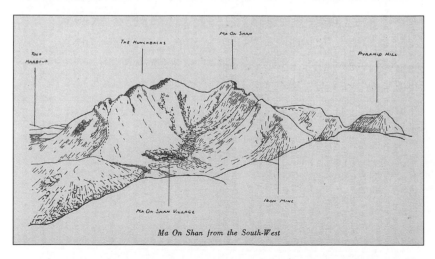

Ma On Shan from the South-West

Recent photographs

Above: Site of the POW Camp: part of it has become Sham Shui Po Park *[34]*
Below: Plaques with trees planted at Sham Shui Po Park by the Hong Kong
Prisoners of War Association and the Hong Kong Veterans Association of
Canada *[35]*

Above: Plaque laid by the Hong Kong Prisoners of War Association *[36]*
Below: One of the three remaining boundary stones of the Sham Shui Po
military camp ("M.O.D." stands for "Ministry of Defence"; "B.S." stands for
"Boundary Stone") *[37]*

Above: Plaque laid by the Hong Kong Veterans Association of Canada *[38]*
Below: Veronica Heywood visiting the Hong Kong Observatory in November
2013, with Shun Chi Ming (left) and Geoffrey Emerson (right)

Above: Veronica Heywood with Lau Tin Chi in the Director's quarters in November 2013; Below: Veronica and Michael Knight at Critchells, Hampshire, February 2015 (the watercolour behind is of Graham Heywood's mother, Mary (nee Stanhope), and her brother in the apple orchard) *[40]*

Above: Graham Heywood's past residence at Critchells, Hampshire *[39]*
Below: Michael Knight and Shun Chi Ming at Winchester College, February
2015 *[41]*

CREDITS

Unless otherwise stated, photographs and images used in this book were either provided by the Heywood family or obtained from the website of the Hong Kong Observatory. The numbers indicate those labelled in the caption of the respective photograph or image.

1, 10, 14, 21, 22: Dr William TONG Cheuk Man

2: LAU Tin Chi

3 to 8, 11 to 13, 17, 23, 26, 27: Tim KO Tim Keung

9, 16, 19, 34 to 41: SHUN Chi Ming

15: *www.gwulo.com*

18: SIU Him Fung

20: James NG Pong Mau

24: *http://en.wikipedia.org/wiki/Stanley_Internment_Camp*

25: Jack Hawes, Department of National Defence, Canada

29: Ricky YAM Ching Chuen

30: *http://en.wikipedia.org/wiki/HMS_Glengyle*

31: The Late Allan Green Victoria Australia Collection & Don Ross Collection

32: Veronica Heywood

EXPLORE ASIA WITH BLACKSMITH BOOKS

From retailers around the world or from *www.blacksmithbooks.com*

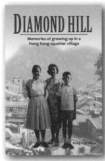

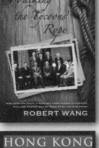

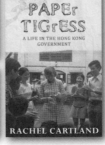